The Enchanted Advent

The Enchanted Advent

Matthew Petchinsky

It's Christmas Time!

The Enchanted Advent: 36 Days of Christmas Wonders
By: Matthew Petchinsky

Introduction: The Magic of Christmas

As the year winds down, a quiet magic fills the air. The days grow shorter, the nights stretch longer, and the world becomes wrapped in a blanket of cold, crisp beauty. This is the time of Christmas, a season unlike any other, imbued with traditions, myths, and a spirit that captivates hearts across the globe. In every corner of the world, Christmas is celebrated in unique ways, with customs that have been passed down through generations. These rituals, whether grand or humble, are steeped in a sense of wonder and warmth that connects people, transcending borders and cultures.

The Magic of Christmas Traditions

Christmas is a tapestry woven from diverse traditions, each one a thread of history, folklore, and familial love. In some places, it is marked by the sound of church bells echoing through a snowy landscape, while in others, it is a time of vibrant feasts and joyful gatherings. Countries like Sweden honor the season with the celebration of *St. Lucia's Day*, where young girls wear crowns of candles, symbolizing the triumph of light over darkness. In Mexico, the lively tradition of *Las Posadas* reenacts Mary and Joseph's search for shelter, ending in a festive celebration filled with music, piñatas, and feasting.

Across Europe, the centuries-old tradition of Christmas markets transforms towns into twinkling wonderlands, where the scent of mulled wine and roasted chestnuts fills the air. These markets, often adorned with handcrafted ornaments and sparkling lights, echo the spirit of an era when Christmas was celebrated with simple joys and communal warmth. Meanwhile, in Japan, Christmas has become a time of romantic dates and festive illuminations, a season of love that finds new expression amidst the neon-lit cityscapes.

Then there is the figure of Santa Claus, known by many names: *Saint Nicholas, Father Christmas, Père Noël,* and *Kris Kringle,* to name a few. His legend is a blend of myths and stories that span continents, from the kindly bishop of Myra who became the patron saint of children, to the jolly, gift-bearing figure who traverses the globe in a single night. His presence embodies the essence of giving, joy, and the belief that, even in the coldest, darkest winter, there is warmth and light to be found.

Christmas Myths and Legends

Beneath the surface of cheerful carols and festive decorations lie tales of magic and mystery that have enchanted people for centuries. In Norse mythology, the *Yule* season was marked by the *Wild Hunt*, a spectral chase across the winter skies led by the god Odin. This ancient celebration, rooted in the pagan customs of Scandinavia, is where many modern-day Christmas symbols like the Yule log originate. The act of bringing greenery indoors—holly, ivy, and the evergreen tree—is a vestige of these rituals, a way of honoring nature's resilience during the bleak winter months.

In Central Europe, the ominous figure of *Krampus* roams through Christmas folklore, a horned creature who punishes misbehaving children while *St. Nicholas* rewards the good. His story serves as a reminder of the dual nature of the season: joy mingled with caution, light interwoven with shadow. Meanwhile, in Celtic traditions, tales of the *Winter Solstice* speak of the rebirth of the sun and the defeat of darkness, themes that resonate deeply in the story of Christmas itself.

The Premise of the Book: 36 Days of Christmas Wonders

This book is a journey through the 36 days leading up to Christmas—a season that begins long before December 25th and extends into the New Year. Each day will uncover a new layer of Christmas, offering readers a unique blend of stories, recipes, crafts, and activities that evoke the spirit of the season. Some chapters delve into ancient myths and legends, drawing from the magical lore that surrounds Christmas. Others explore customs and traditions from around the world, showcasing how this holiday is celebrated in diverse and beautiful ways.

You will encounter tales of winter wonders, from enchanted forests to mystical reindeer, and join in festive feasts filled with family recipes passed down through generations. You will uncover the secrets of snowflakes, explore the history of the Christmas market, and even step into the world of Christmas spirits—both joyful and eerie. Along the way, you'll find inspiration for your own holiday season, whether through crafting homemade gifts, cooking traditional dishes, or simply embracing the quiet magic of a winter's night.

This book is designed to be more than just a collection of holiday lore. It is an invitation to immerse yourself in the magic of Christmas, to create memories and traditions that will linger long after the final snow has melted. The chapters are crafted to spark your imagination, to provide moments of reflection, and to fill each day with a small dose of wonder and joy. From the first snowfall to the glimmering lights of Christmas morning, every page offers a new way to celebrate and cherish the spirit of the season.

As you journey through these 36 days, you may find that the magic of Christmas isn't confined to a single day on the calendar. It lives in the stories we tell, the love we share, and the warmth we create amidst the winter chill. It's in the simple act of hanging an ornament, baking a batch of cookies, or watching the soft glow of candlelight. Most importantly, it's in the anticipation—the feeling that something special is unfolding, moment by moment, leading us toward a day that is as much about giving as it is about gathering together and finding joy in one another.

So, turn the page, and let us begin this journey. May it bring a touch of magic to your heart, a sparkle to your eyes, and a reminder that Christmas is more than just a date on the calendar—it's a season of wonder that lives within us all. Welcome to the *Enchanted Advent,* where each day reveals a new delight, guiding you through the enchanting days of Christmas.

Part 1: *Winter Whispers: The Advent of Christmas Magic*

Chapter 1: The First Snow

As autumn draws to a close and the last leaves fall to the ground, there comes a moment when the air turns crisp, filled with the scent of pine and woodsmoke. On this night, the world seems to hold its breath, awaiting a transformation—a change from the amber hues of fall to the silvery wonderland of winter. And then, almost as if by magic, it happens. Tiny crystals begin to descend from the heavens, each one unique and delicate. It is the first snow of the season, a spectacle that has captivated hearts and imaginations for generations. But what if this snowfall wasn't just a weather phenomenon, but a moment steeped in magic and myth?

The First Snow: A Tale from the Whispering Forest

Long ago, in the farthest reaches of the north, there was a place known as the Whispering Forest, a realm where magic still lingered in the roots of ancient trees and in the winds that danced through the branches. The forest was said to be home to all manner of mystical creatures: wise old owls who carried secrets, mischievous foxes who could vanish into thin air, and faeries whose laughter rang like the soft chime of bells. But the most revered of all was the *Snow Weaver*, a spirit older than the forest itself.

The Snow Weaver was a guardian of winter, an ethereal being who lived deep within the forest in a crystalline palace that shimmered with frost. She awoke from her slumber each year at the cusp of winter, her long silvery hair flowing behind her like a veil of moonlight. Her eyes, the color of ice, could see into the hearts of all creatures, discerning whether they had carried the warmth of kindness throughout the year.

It was said that the first snow of the season was no mere accident of weather but rather the work of the Snow Weaver herself. As the story goes, she would emerge from her palace on the night of the first frost, carrying a spindle woven from the branches of the oldest tree in the forest. The spindle held the threads of winter—a mixture of starlight, frost, and whispers of the wind.

Under the cover of darkness, the Snow Weaver would spin these threads into snowflakes, each one different from the last. She worked tirelessly, her hands moving with a grace and speed that could only belong to a being of magic. When her task was finished, she would climb to the highest peak in the forest, hold her hands to the sky, and release the snowflakes into the wind. With a gentle breath, she would send them spiraling down to the earth, marking the beginning of winter.

As the snowflakes fell, they whispered secrets to those who listened—tales of ancient times, of forgotten magic, and of the cycles of nature that continue, year after year. It was said that if you caught a snowflake on the night of the first snow and held it close, you could hear these whispers, the voice of the Snow Weaver herself, telling you of the mysteries that lie hidden in the world.

The Snow's Blessing

The first snow was more than just a herald of winter; it was a blessing, a sign that the world was entering a time of rest and reflection. The Snow Weaver's magic infused each snowflake with a sense of peace and renewal, reminding all who witnessed it that even in the coldest, darkest days, beauty and grace could be found. For the creatures of the forest, the first snow was a signal to prepare for the season ahead. The deer, rabbits, and foxes would scurry to find shelter, while the bears would settle into their dens, ready for their long winter's sleep.

In human villages near the forest, the arrival of the first snow was met with reverence. People would gather in the town square, children bundled in woolen coats, their faces glowing with excitement as they watched the sky. When the first flakes began to fall, there would be a hush, a collective intake of breath, as if the entire village were witnessing a miracle. It was a tradition for each family to open their doors, allowing a handful of the first snow to drift inside, symbolizing the welcoming of winter's magic into their homes.

Elders would tell tales by the fireside, passing down the legend of the Snow Weaver and her gift. They would explain how, on the night of the first snow, you must make a wish, for it was believed that the Snow Weaver would carry the wishes of the pure-hearted on the winds. The wishes would be wrapped in snowflakes, to be woven into the fabric of winter itself. And if the Snow Weaver deemed your heart true, your wish would come to pass before the winter ended.

The Mythical Origins of Snow

The story of the Snow Weaver is but one of many myths surrounding the first snow of the season. Across the world, various cultures have created their own legends to explain this magical occurrence. In ancient Norse mythology, the first snow was thought to be the breath of the goddess *Skadi*, the deity of winter and mountains. She would descend from the peaks to blanket the earth in frost, a reminder of her power and the harsh beauty of winter.

In the folklore of the Celtic lands, it was believed that snow came from the *Caillach Bheur*, the Winter Hag who ruled over the cold months. On the night of the first snow, the Caillach would take her great white staff and strike the ground, turning everything she touched into ice and snow. This act was seen as her way of claiming the land, marking it as her domain until the spring thaw.

Even in the East, where snow is less frequent, legends tell of celestial dragons that breathe snow down upon the earth. The first snow was considered a sign of favor from these dragons, a blessing of protection for the villages below. In these cultures, families would make offerings of rice and tea, leaving them on their doorsteps to thank the dragons for their gift.

The Magic of Today

Though the ancient myths and legends have faded into the background in our modern world, the magic of the first snow remains. There is still a sense of wonder that comes with the sight of those first few flakes drifting silently from the sky. It is a moment that invites us to pause, to watch, and to listen, as if the world is whispering secrets in a language only snow can speak.

Perhaps, on the night of the first snow this year, you might step outside, tilt your head to the sky, and catch a snowflake on your tongue. And as it melts, let it remind you of the stories of old, of the Snow Weaver spinning her threads of winter, of the dragons, and the winter hags. Let it be a moment of reflection, a reminder that even in the quiet, cold embrace of winter, there is magic and warmth to be found.

So, as you begin this journey through the 36 days of Christmas wonders, let the first snow mark your entry into the season of magic. Whether it arrives early or late, heavy or light, may it fill your heart with the age-old promise of winter: that in the silence and stillness, beauty and joy await.

Activity: Catching the First Snow

When you experience the first snowfall of the season, take a moment to capture its magic. Find a quiet place outside and hold out your hand, letting the snowflakes land on your palm. Close your eyes and make a wish, something dear to your heart. Remember the legend of the Snow Weaver and believe, even if only for a moment, that your wish might be carried away on the whispering winds of winter.

If you have children or friends with you, share the legend and encourage them to make their own wishes. It's a simple act, but one that brings a touch of magic to the beginning of the Christmas season. For the young and the young at heart, it serves as a reminder that there is beauty in nature, and that the first snow is more than just a change in weather—it's an age-old dance of magic and myth.

Chapter 2: The Wishing Tree

The Christmas tree, with its twinkling lights and shimmering ornaments, stands as one of the most cherished symbols of the holiday season. Its presence transforms homes, filling them with the scent of fresh pine and the warmth of nostalgia. But the Christmas tree is more than just a festive decoration; it is steeped in ancient myths and legends that speak of a time when the tree itself was seen as a conduit for wishes and magic. In this chapter, we will explore the legend of the Wishing Tree—a tale that tells of enchanted trees that hold the power to grant the deepest desires of the heart.

The Ancient Origins of the Wishing Tree

Long before Christmas trees graced living rooms with their splendor, the evergreen tree was regarded as a sacred symbol in many cultures. In ancient times, the people of northern Europe revered the mighty pine, fir, and spruce as trees of life. Their evergreen needles represented resilience and endurance, remaining lush and green even during the harshest winters. These trees were thought to harbor the spirits of nature, and during the midwinter solstice, people would decorate them with symbols of life—fruits, nuts, and candles—to honor these spirits and ensure a prosperous year ahead.

The legend of the Wishing Tree has roots in these ancient practices. According to folklore, there was a time when the forests were home to magical trees known as *Yuldrassils*, named after the Norse *Yggdrasil*, the great tree that connects all realms of existence. These Yuldrassils were rare and elusive, hidden deep within enchanted groves where only the pure of heart could find them. It was said that these trees glowed softly in the moonlight, their branches adorned with tiny icicles that sparkled like stars.

The Yuldrassils were believed to possess a unique power: they could hear the whispers of wishes carried on the winter wind. On the night of the winter solstice, when the veil between the worlds was thinnest, these trees would awaken. Their branches would sway and rustle, not from the wind but from the stirring of magic within them. During this time, the Yuldrassils would grant one wish to each person who came to them with a true and selfless heart.

The First Wishing Tree: A Tale of Hope and Light

The most famous legend of the Wishing Tree dates back to a time when a small village nestled at the edge of a vast, snow-covered forest faced a harsh winter. The villagers were poor and hungry, struggling to keep warm as the cold winds howled through their humble homes. Among them was a young girl named Elara, whose kindness and generosity had endeared her to everyone in the village.

Elara's father had fallen ill, and the family's small stockpile of food was dwindling. Despite their hardships, Elara shared what little they had with neighbors who were even worse off, believing that kindness was the truest form of strength. As the winter solstice approached, Elara heard the elders speak of the Yuldrassil, the Wishing Tree hidden deep in the forest. The story told that if one approached the tree on the solstice night and spoke a wish with a heart full of love, the tree would grant it.

Desperate to help her family and village, Elara decided to seek the Wishing Tree. On the night of the solstice, she ventured into the forest, guided only by the light of the full moon. The snow crunched softly under her feet, and the air was filled with an otherworldly stillness. As she wandered deeper into the woods, she began to doubt the legend. How could a tree possibly grant wishes? But just as she was about to turn back, a soft glow appeared in the distance.

Elara approached cautiously, and there it stood—the Yuldrassil. Its branches were heavy with snow, yet it emitted a soft, golden light. The icicles that hung from its limbs sparkled like a thousand tiny stars. Heart pounding, she stepped forward, knelt at the base of the tree, and whispered her wish: "Please, bring warmth and hope to my village. Help us through this winter."

For a moment, nothing happened. Then, a gust of wind swept through the clearing, rustling the tree's branches. The air grew warmer, and as Elara looked up, she saw a single star-shaped snowflake descending toward her. It landed gently in her hand, melting into a droplet that glowed briefly before disappearing. Elara felt a surge of hope in her heart. She thanked the tree and made her way back to the village.

The next morning, the villagers awoke to find the forest brimming with life. Despite the deep winter, they discovered that the trees around the village were laden with berries and nuts, and the streams, which had been frozen solid, were flowing with fresh, clear water. Miraculously, their homes seemed warmer, the air filled with a sense of peace and renewal. Word spread of Elara's encounter with the Wishing Tree, and from that day forward, the villagers honored the evergreen as a tree of hope, decorating it each year to celebrate its magical blessing.

The Christmas Tree Tradition

As the legend of the Wishing Tree spread across the land, the tradition of bringing evergreen trees into homes began to take shape. People believed that by inviting a tree into their homes, they were bringing a piece of the forest's magic with them. They would adorn these trees with candles, fruits, and small trinkets as offerings to the spirits of nature and to the memory of the Yuldrassil. Over time, this practice evolved into what we now recognize as the Christmas tree, a symbol of life, light, and the power of wishes.

In various cultures, the tradition of the Wishing Tree took on different forms. In Germany, it became customary to hang apples and nuts on the tree, symbols of the abundance they hoped to receive in the coming year. In Eastern Europe, people would place golden stars atop their trees, representing the star-shaped snowflakes from the legend and the wishes they carried. In modern times, ornaments of every shape and color adorn Christmas trees, each one a reminder of the magic of the season and the hopes and dreams we hold dear.

The Enchantment of the Tree Today

Though the myth of the Yuldrassil has faded into the realm of folklore, the tradition of the Christmas tree continues to be filled with enchantment. Today, many families partake in the custom of making wishes as they decorate their trees. Some write their wishes on slips of paper and tuck them into ornaments, while others place a special wish star on the top of the tree, believing that it will carry their hopes to the heavens.

The act of gathering around the tree, hanging ornaments, and lighting its branches is more than just a festive ritual; it is an unspoken acknowledgment of the power of wishes and the magic that resides in hope. Each ornament tells a story, each light a beacon of warmth and joy that chases away the darkness of winter. In this way, the Christmas tree becomes a modern-day Wishing Tree, a symbol of the season's magic and the belief that wishes, spoken from the heart, can indeed come true.

Activity: Creating Your Own Wishing Tree

This year, as you decorate your Christmas tree, why not turn it into a Wishing Tree for you and your family? Here's how to capture the magic of the ancient legend:

1. **Gather Supplies**: You will need slips of paper, ribbons, pens, and a small box or pouch. If you have a star ornament, set it aside for later.

2. **Make Your Wishes**: Gather your family around the tree. Have each person take a slip of paper and write down a wish for the season or the coming year. The wish can be for themselves, their family, friends, or even the world.

3. **Tuck Away the Wishes**: Roll up each slip of paper and tie it with a ribbon. Hide the wishes within the branches of the tree, securing them among the ornaments and lights.

4. **The Wish Star**: Once all the wishes have been placed on the tree, take the star ornament and place it on the top of the tree. As you do, say a simple blessing or wish for all the hopes hidden within the tree to be heard and granted.

5. **Keep the Magic Alive**: At the end of the Christmas season, gather the wishes from the tree. Keep them in a special box to reflect upon during the next year's festivities.

This simple activity not only connects us to the ancient myths of the Wishing Tree but also serves as a reminder that the magic of Christmas lies in the wishes and dreams we hold close. And who knows? Perhaps the spirit of the Yuldrassil still listens, carrying our wishes on the winds of winter, just as it did long ago.

Chapter 3: Elves' Secret Workshop

Tucked away in the frozen wilderness of the North Pole, where the auroras dance across the sky and the snow glistens like millions of diamonds, lies one of the greatest secrets of Christmas: Santa's workshop. To the untrained eye, it appears to be a humble cluster of log cabins and stone chimneys nestled between towering pines. But for those lucky enough to see it, the workshop is a realm of wonder, a place where magic and craftsmanship come together to create the joy of Christmas. And at the heart of this incredible workshop are Santa's elves—the industrious, mystical, and mischievous creatures who make the magic of Christmas possible.

This chapter opens the door to the world of the elves, taking us behind the scenes to reveal the secrets of Santa's workshop. From the stories of how it came to be, to the enchanted creatures and wondrous machines that bring toys to life, we delve into the myths and marvels of this extraordinary place.

The Origin of the Elves' Workshop

Long before Santa Claus became the jolly, gift-giving figure we know today, the northern lands were said to be inhabited by a race of magical beings known as the *Nisse* and *Tomte* in Scandinavian folklore. These creatures, small in stature but mighty in spirit, were guardians of hearth and home, watching over farms and families throughout the year. As the stories go, they would help with daily chores and protect the household, but in return, they demanded respect and offerings of food, especially during the long, dark winters.

Over centuries, as tales of Saint Nicholas spread and evolved, the legend of Santa Claus emerged. According to the myth, when Saint Nicholas decided to make his permanent home in the North Pole to bring joy to children all over the world, he befriended these guardian creatures. In exchange for their service in his new venture, he promised to share with them the magic of Christmas, a powerful enchantment that would keep them young, joyous, and full of life. Thus, the Nisse and Tomte transformed into Santa's elves, becoming his loyal helpers in the grand endeavor of spreading cheer to children everywhere.

The Hidden Realm of the Workshop

Santa's workshop is unlike any other place in the world. Surrounded by an impenetrable blizzard, the North Pole is shrouded in an eternal winter. Only those with a pure heart and a sprinkle of Christmas magic can find their way to the workshop, which is protected by ancient spells cast by the elves. As you step inside, the blizzard's howl fades, replaced by the sound of laughter, music, and the steady rhythm of crafting tools.

The workshop itself is a sprawling complex of interconnected buildings, each serving a different purpose. Its main hall, known as the *Hall of Crafts*, is a vast chamber filled with rows upon rows of wooden workbenches. Here, hundreds of elves gather to create toys using tools that seem ordinary but hum with an inner magic. At one end of the hall, a massive fireplace crackles with enchanted flames that never burn out, keeping the entire room warm and cozy despite the frigid temperatures outside.

The Elves: The Heart of the Workshop

The elves are the lifeblood of Santa's operation. Standing no taller than three feet, they are agile and nimble, with pointed ears, twinkling eyes, and faces that always seem on the verge of laughter. Each elf possesses a unique talent, and their roles within the workshop reflect this diversity.

- **The Master Toymakers** are the most skilled of the elves, responsible for crafting the toys that will fill Santa's sleigh. They specialize in woodworking, metal crafting, and painting, imbuing each creation with an essence of joy. These elves work with remarkable speed and precision, their hands moving in a blur as they carve, mold, and assemble. The toy they cherish most is the rocking horse, which they say captures the spirit of childhood adventure.

- **The Enchanting Elves** handle the delicate art of imbuing toys with magic. In a corner of the workshop known as the *Chamber of Spells*, these elves mix potions, grind stardust, and whisper incantations over each toy, breathing life into stuffed animals, animating toy soldiers, and ensuring that dolls open their eyes with a sparkle of mischief. The Enchanting Elves are known for their secretive ways, guarding their spells closely and speaking in a language that sounds like a mix of bells and wind chimes.

- **The Wrapping Wizards** are the artists behind the beautifully wrapped presents that Santa delivers. With ribbons that tie themselves and paper that changes color depending on the recipient's favorite hue, these elves turn each gift into a masterpiece. They believe that a beautifully wrapped present is the first hint of the magic within, and they take great pride in their craft.

- **The Map Keepers** are responsible for Santa's route on Christmas Eve. In a room filled with celestial maps and charts, these elves study the stars and track weather patterns across the globe.

They use ancient compasses and enchanted sextants to plot Santa's course, ensuring that he reaches every child in one magical night. Legend says they work closely with the North Star, which shines brighter than ever on Christmas Eve to guide Santa on his journey.

The Magical Creatures of the Workshop

The elves are not alone in their work; they are assisted by an array of enchanted creatures that inhabit the workshop grounds. Chief among them are the *Snow Hares*, magical rabbits with fur as white as snow and eyes that gleam with intelligence. They help transport supplies from one part of the workshop to another, zipping through the snow-covered courtyards with small sleds attached to their backs.

There are also the *Glimmer Pixies*, tiny glowing sprites that flit about the workshop, bringing light to the darkest corners and adding a touch of magic to every project. The elves rely on these pixies to keep their spirits high during the long nights of winter, and it is said that a sprinkle of pixie dust can make even the most challenging toy come to life.

Perhaps the most unusual helpers in the workshop are the *Aurora Bears*, massive but gentle creatures whose fur shimmers with the colors of the Northern Lights. These bears help transport the completed toys to Santa's sleigh on Christmas Eve. Despite their size, they move with the grace of a soft winter breeze, ensuring that every toy is safely loaded for the journey ahead.

The Secrets of Toy Making

The toy-making process in Santa's workshop is a blend of skill, magic, and tradition passed down through generations of elves. The elves begin their work months in advance, using only the finest materials sourced from the enchanted North Pole forests. The wood for toy trains, blocks, and rocking horses comes from the *Evergreen Oaks*, trees that absorb the joy of the winter season and retain the essence of childhood wonder in their grain.

Once the toys are carved and shaped, they are taken to the Chamber of Spells, where the Enchanting Elves work their magic. A special mixture of *starlight ink* is used to paint the toys, giving them a sheen that catches the eye. This ink, harvested from the stars that fall during the first winter snows, is said to contain the dreams of children. As the elves paint and decorate, they whisper the names of the children who will receive each toy, ensuring that every gift is perfectly suited to its recipient.

In the final stage, the Wrapping Wizards take over, swathing the toys in vibrant paper and ribbons. They tie each package with a special knot known as the *Elf's Bow*, which, when untied, releases a faint jingling sound—like the echo of sleigh bells on a winter's night. The wrapped gifts are then placed in a special *Starlight Sack*, an enchanted bag that keeps the presents hidden until Christmas Eve.

A Day in the Life of an Elf

The elves' days are filled with work, but it is work they love. They wake with the first light of dawn, which, in the North Pole, casts a soft pink hue across the snow. After a hearty breakfast of *Yuleberry Porridge*—a magical dish that keeps them energized all day—they gather in the workshop, where laughter and music fill the air. Though they are industrious, they are never too busy to share a joke, sing a song, or lend a hand to a fellow elf.

As night falls, they take a break from their work to gather in the *Hall of Lights*, a grand chamber illuminated by thousands of twinkling candles. Here, they celebrate the joy of their labor, recounting stories of the toys they have made and the children they will bring joy to. It is during these moments that they recharge their own magic, drawing strength from their camaraderie and the knowledge that they are part of something greater than themselves.

Activity: Elf-Inspired Toy Crafting

To experience a touch of the elves' magic, try your hand at making a simple toy inspired by the workshop's traditions. One of the elves' favorite crafts is the *Wish Star Ornament*, a sparkling decoration that can hold a secret wish.

1. **Materials**: You will need a small star-shaped ornament (wood, cardboard, or felt), glitter or metallic paint, a small piece of paper, and ribbon.

2. **Create Your Star**: Paint or decorate the star ornament with glitter, making it shine like the stars over the North Pole. As you work, think of the magic the elves put into their toys, and infuse your ornament with joy and hope.

3. **Add a Wish**: Write a wish or a positive intention on the piece of paper, fold it tightly, and tuck it inside the ornament or attach it to the back with ribbon. This is your personal touch of magic, just like the elves whispering the names of children into their toys.

4. **Hang It Up**: Place your Wish Star on your Christmas tree, a reminder of the elves' workshop and the magic that fills each holiday season.

The elves' workshop, with its enchantment and endless joy, stands as a testament to the spirit of Christmas. Each toy they craft is more than just an object—it is a vessel of dreams, a symbol of hope, and a spark of magic that travels from the North Pole to every corner of the world. By sharing in the elves' secrets, we too can become part of this wondrous tradition, bringing a little bit of their magic into our own homes and hearts.

Chapter 4: Letters to the North Pole

For generations, children around the world have penned their hopes and dreams on pieces of paper and sent them to the most magical address on Earth: the North Pole. These letters to Santa Claus are not merely wish lists; they are a cherished tradition, a conduit for the joy, wonder, and belief that define the Christmas season. In this chapter, we will explore the art of writing Christmas letters, the history behind this heartwarming custom, and how this simple act has become a symbol of hope, kindness, and the magic of the season. Along the way, we'll look at real-life examples of letters, showcasing the innocence, sincerity, and charm found in each one.

The Origins of Christmas Letters

The tradition of writing letters to Santa Claus has its roots in ancient customs and folklore. In the early days, children would place their wishes near the hearth or in their shoes, believing that the magical beings of winter—whether elves, fairies, or the spirit of Saint Nicholas—would find them. As the legend of Santa Claus grew and spread across the world, the act of writing letters became an integral part of the Christmas season.

By the 19th century, children in many cultures had begun to write their Christmas wishes on paper, which they would then either burn in the fireplace (so that their wishes could ascend to the North Pole in the smoke) or place in the mail. The first documented letter to Santa Claus in the United States appeared in the 1870s, marking the beginning of a heartfelt tradition that continues to this day.

Over time, the idea of Santa receiving and reading each letter became a magical cornerstone of the holiday. Santa's workshop at the North Pole transformed into a bustling post office, where elves sorted through mountains of letters from around the world, ensuring that each child's wishes were heard. The letters were filled not just with requests for toys but also with messages of gratitude, kindness, and sometimes even promises to be good in the coming year.

The Art of Writing to Santa

Writing a letter to Santa is more than just listing the items one hopes to receive on Christmas morning. It is an expression of belief in the magic of Christmas and an opportunity to reflect on the year that has passed. A good Christmas letter has a few key elements that bring it to life: a personal greeting to Santa, a brief recap of the year, a thoughtful wish list, and, most importantly, a message of gratitude and goodwill. Here's a guide to crafting the perfect letter to Santa:

1. **Greeting Santa**: Start your letter with a warm greeting. Santa is not just a mythical figure; he is the embodiment of generosity and kindness. Address him as you would an old friend: "Dear Santa," or "Hello, Santa Claus!" This simple salutation sets the tone for a heartfelt letter.

2. **Sharing the Year's Highlights**: In your letter, take a moment to reflect on the past year. This is your chance to tell Santa about the good things that have happened, the challenges you've overcome, or how you've been trying to be kind and helpful. It doesn't have to be lengthy; even a short summary provides a glimpse into your personal journey and makes the letter more meaningful.

3. **The Wish List**: When it comes to the wish list, be thoughtful and honest. Children often ask for the toys they desire most, but they may also include wishes for their family, friends, or even the world. Encourage adding a mix of personal wishes and wishes that extend kindness to others. This shows Santa that they are thinking beyond just themselves, embracing the true spirit of Christmas.

4. **Messages of Gratitude and Goodwill**: Conclude your letter with words of gratitude. Thank Santa for all he does, for the magic he brings to Christmas, and for reading your letter. It's also a nice touch to wish him, Mrs. Claus, and the elves a happy

Christmas. This simple gesture reflects the essence of Christmas: giving thanks and spreading joy.

5. **The Signature**: End with your name and age, and perhaps a short closing line like "Love," "Warmly," or "Your friend." Adding age is a sweet touch, giving Santa a little insight into the writer.

Real-Life Examples of Christmas Letters

Here are some examples of Christmas letters that capture the innocence and charm of this tradition, showing the different ways children express themselves to Santa:

Example 1: The Thoughtful Letter

"Dear Santa Claus,

This year has been really good. I helped my little sister learn to read, and I tried to do my chores without being asked. For Christmas, I would love a new bike so I can ride to school. But I also wish for my grandpa to get better because he has been sick. Thank you for always bringing happiness to our house. I hope you and Mrs. Claus are doing well. Please give the elves a big hug from me!

Love, Lily (age 8)"

This letter shows a thoughtful approach, blending personal wishes with kindness for family and gratitude towards Santa and his helpers. It embodies the warmth and love that Christmas inspires.

Example 2: The Simple, Heartfelt Letter

"Hi Santa,

How are you? I have been trying to be good. I would like a teddy bear, a book, and some crayons. I will leave cookies and milk for you. Please say hi to the reindeer!

From, Jack (age 5)"

Short and sweet, this letter captures the simplicity of a child's wish, accompanied by the excitement and anticipation that Christmas brings. It may be brief, but it's full of sincerity.

Example 3: The Generous Wish

"Dear Santa Claus,

Thank you for all the toys you brought last year. This Christmas, I would like a puzzle and some art supplies. Also, can you please bring a warm blanket for my friend in school because he doesn't have one? I think he would really like it. Thank you for making Christmas so special. I will leave carrots for the reindeer too!

Sincerely, Emma (age 9)"

Here, Emma not only asks for gifts for herself but also includes a generous wish for someone else. It is a beautiful reminder of the spirit of giving that Christmas encourages.

Creating a Magical Response

For those who wish to take the tradition a step further, responding to the letters adds an extra layer of magic. A reply from "Santa" can be a memorable keepsake for children, reinforcing the belief that their words matter and that kindness is always noticed.

To craft a Santa response, follow these guidelines:

- Begin with a cheerful greeting: "Ho Ho Ho! Merry Christmas, [Name]!"
- Acknowledge something specific from the child's letter to show that Santa has read and cared about what they shared.
- Include a brief update from the North Pole, such as how the elves are preparing or how the reindeer are training for their big flight.
- Offer encouragement and praise for good behavior or efforts the child has made during the year.
- Conclude with warm wishes, promising to do your best to deliver joy on Christmas Eve.

The Legacy of Christmas Letters

The tradition of writing letters to Santa is more than a way for children to ask for gifts. It is an exercise in hope, imagination, and generosity. These letters become a part of the lore of Christmas, preserved in hearts and memories long after the holiday has passed. In writing their letters, children practice the art of self-expression, reflect on their own behavior, and learn to articulate their wishes and dreams.

In some cultures, special mailboxes are set up in town squares for children to post their letters to the North Pole. In others, families create their own ritual of placing the letters in the fireplace, watching the smoke curl upward as a symbol of their wishes traveling to Santa. And in recent years, technology has added a modern twist, with children emailing or using Santa apps to send their letters. Regardless of the method, the essence remains the same: the belief that wishes can reach Santa and that kindness will be rewarded.

Activity: Writing Your Own Letter to Santa

Set aside an evening to write your Christmas letter. Gather around the table with family, bring out stationery, markers, stickers, and anything that can make your letter unique. Follow the steps outlined in this chapter to create a heartfelt letter. Here are some prompts to get you started:

- "What is one thing you did this year that made you proud?"
- "Who is someone you would like to wish for this Christmas, and why?"
- "What is one way you will spread Christmas cheer this holiday season?"

Once you've finished, consider how you want to send your letter. Will you place it in a special mailbox, mail it to the North Pole, or keep it on the windowsill for an elf to collect? If you're writing with children, use this moment to talk about the importance of kindness, giving, and gratitude, reinforcing the values that make Christmas so magical.

A Final Note

The simple act of writing a letter to Santa is a magical ritual that captures the spirit of Christmas. It is a reminder that, even in a world of instant communication and digital everything, the written word still holds the power to express wishes, dreams, and the warmth of human connection. Whether filled with requests for toys, hopes for family, or wishes for a better world, these letters are treasures that embody the magic and love that Christmas brings.

Chapter 5: The Lost Christmas Star

The days leading up to Christmas were always filled with a special kind of magic. The air was crisp, carrying the scent of pine and snow, and everywhere people were bustling about, decorating their homes with twinkling lights, garlands, and ornaments. But in the small, snow-covered village of Winterhaven, something was different this year. It was as if the magic of Christmas had faded slightly, and a soft gloom hung over the town. Children who usually ran with joy now walked with a sense of unease, and even the evergreen trees lining the village square seemed to droop under the weight of their snow-covered branches.

The villagers whispered to each other about what might be wrong. Some said it was the bitter cold, others blamed the unusual quietness in the air. But the oldest among them knew the truth: the Christmas Star was missing.

The Legend of the Christmas Star

Winterhaven was built around a legend as old as time itself. It was said that every Christmas season, a magical star appeared in the sky, filling the town with light, warmth, and joy. This star, known as the *Christmas Star*, was no ordinary celestial body. It was a beacon of hope and a harbinger of the magic that made Christmas so special. The star's glow blessed the village, helping families and friends come together in the spirit of giving, sharing, and love.

But if the star were ever to go missing, the magic of Christmas would weaken. The season would feel darker and colder, and the joy that normally spread so easily would become harder to find. For centuries, the Christmas Star had shone without fail, lighting up the hearts of the villagers. However, this year, it had disappeared, leaving nothing but the bleak winter night behind.

The Call for Adventure

Among the villagers was a young boy named Finn. He was small and nimble, with bright eyes that sparkled with curiosity and courage. Finn had always loved Christmas, not just for the presents or the delicious food but for the warmth and love that seemed to fill every corner of Winterhaven when the Christmas Star shone brightly. But now, with the star gone, Finn could sense the sadness in the air, and it filled his heart with a deep resolve. He had to find the Christmas Star and bring its light back to his village.

One evening, as the townspeople gathered in the village square to discuss what to do, Finn stood up, his voice firm yet filled with the innocence of youth. "I will find the Christmas Star!" he declared. The villagers looked at him in surprise, some with concern. He was, after all, just a boy. But there was something in his eyes that made them believe. Perhaps it was the glimmer of determination, or maybe it was the flicker of the Christmas magic that still lived inside him.

After some discussion, the village elders agreed to let Finn go on his quest, though they warned him of the challenges that lay ahead. "The path to the Christmas Star is not easy," said old Grimbald, the town's historian. "You must pass through the *Whispering Woods*, cross the *Frozen River*, and climb the *Frosted Peaks*. Only then will you find the *Cavern of the Lost Star*. But be careful, for many have ventured and never returned."

Undeterred, Finn nodded. The villagers prepared him with warm clothes, food, and a small lantern that glowed with the light of their hopes and prayers. And so, with the first light of dawn, Finn set off on his journey to find the lost Christmas Star.

The Journey Begins: The Whispering Woods

The first part of Finn's journey took him into the Whispering Woods, a forest known for its towering, ancient trees whose branches interlaced overhead, creating a canopy that blocked out the sky. As Finn entered, he heard the woods whispering softly, as if the trees were sharing secrets. The air was thick with mystery, and every rustle of leaves made Finn's heart race. He gripped his lantern tightly, its soft glow the only source of comfort in the darkened woods.

The path was winding and treacherous, filled with hidden roots and snow-covered stones. As he ventured deeper, Finn suddenly heard a faint, melodious voice. "Why do you come, young traveler?" the voice asked, its tone gentle yet echoing through the forest.

"I seek the Christmas Star," Finn replied, his voice steady despite his nerves.

"Many have come before you, seeking the star, but few have succeeded," the voice continued. "The path requires not only courage but also kindness, wisdom, and an open heart."

Finn nodded, remembering the tales the elders had told of the forest. The Whispering Woods tested travelers, revealing their true intentions. Finn walked on, and soon he came upon a clearing where an old, twisted tree stood. Its branches were bare, and at its base sat a small, shivering rabbit.

"Help me," the rabbit squeaked, its tiny body trembling. "I'm lost and cannot find my way back to my burrow."

Finn felt a tug in his heart. He set down his lantern and approached the rabbit. "I will help you," he said gently. Picking up the rabbit, he warmed it in his hands and followed the trails in the snow, soon finding a small burrow beneath the roots of a tree.

"Thank you," the rabbit whispered, its eyes gleaming with gratitude. "You have shown kindness, young traveler. The path ahead will now reveal itself." And with that, the forest seemed to brighten slightly, the shadows receding as a new trail opened before Finn.

The Frozen River

After leaving the woods, Finn came to the edge of the Frozen River, its surface slick with ice. The river was wide and stretched as far as his eyes could see. To cross it seemed impossible. The ice was thin in some places and treacherous to navigate.

As he stood at the edge, contemplating his next move, a voice called out to him from the far side. "You cannot cross the river alone!" it warned. Finn squinted and saw a figure—a fox with fur as white as snow—standing on the opposite bank.

"How can I cross?" Finn shouted back.

"You must trust the ice, but also listen to it," the fox replied. "The river will guide you if you let it."

Taking a deep breath, Finn stepped onto the ice. It creaked and groaned under his weight, but he moved carefully, placing each step with caution. He listened to the sounds beneath his feet, feeling for the places where the ice was solid and where it was thin. Slowly but surely, he made his way across, the fox watching him with keen eyes.

When he reached the other side, the fox bowed its head. "You have shown wisdom, young traveler," it said. "The path to the Frosted Peaks is now open to you." And with a flick of its tail, the fox vanished into the snow, leaving behind a clear path that led towards the mountains.

The Frosted Peaks and the Cavern of the Lost Star

The final part of Finn's journey was the hardest. The Frosted Peaks loomed high above him, their sharp, icy cliffs rising into the clouds. The wind howled, biting at his face as he began the ascent. The climb was steep, and his hands grew numb as he gripped the rocky ledges, pulling himself upward.

Hours passed, and just as exhaustion threatened to overwhelm him, he saw it: a faint glow emanating from a crevice in the mountain. Summoning his last reserves of strength, Finn climbed toward the light. When he reached the top, he found himself standing at the entrance of a vast cavern, its walls glittering with ice crystals. And in the center, on a pedestal of ice, rested the Christmas Star.

The star was more magnificent than he had ever imagined, glowing with a light that shimmered like the northern lights. But as Finn approached, he saw that its light was dim, flickering as though it were struggling to stay alive.

"Why have you come?" the star whispered, its voice faint yet warm.

"I have come to bring you back to Winterhaven," Finn replied, his heart swelling with determination. "The village needs your light."

"To carry me, you must share your light with mine," the star said. "Only through the warmth of your heart can I shine once more."

Finn nodded, reaching out his hand. As he touched the star, a surge of warmth filled him. It was as though all the kindness, courage, and hope he had gathered on his journey flowed from his heart into the star. Slowly, its light grew stronger, radiating outward until the entire cavern was bathed in a golden glow.

With the star now glowing brightly in his hands, Finn made his way back down the mountain. The path that had seemed so perilous before now felt light and easy, as though the star itself was guiding his steps.

The Return to Winterhaven

When Finn finally returned to the village, the townspeople gathered, gasping in awe at the sight of the glowing star. With a steady hand, Finn placed the Christmas Star atop the grand fir tree in the village square. Immediately, the star's light burst forth, filling every corner of Winterhaven with warmth and joy. The gloom lifted, and the magic of Christmas returned, spreading smiles and laughter among the villagers.

"You did it, Finn!" they cheered, lifting him onto their shoulders. The village square came alive with celebration, the air filled with music and the sweet scent of holiday treats.

As Finn looked up at the shining star, he felt a profound sense of peace. The journey had been long and difficult, but through kindness, wisdom, and the courage to face the unknown, he had brought the light of the Christmas Star back to Winterhaven. And with its return, the spirit of Christmas was rekindled in every heart.

From that day on, the story of the Lost Christmas Star was told every year in Winterhaven. It became a reminder that the light of Christmas is not just found in the stars above but also in the kindness, bravery, and love within each of us. And every Christmas Eve, when the star shone its brightest, the villagers would look up and remember the young boy who ventured into the unknown to bring the magic of Christmas back to their lives.

Activity: Making Your Own Christmas Star

To capture a bit of the magic from Finn's adventure, create your own Christmas Star to hang on your tree.

1. **Materials Needed**: A star-shaped ornament or piece of sturdy cardboard cut into a star shape, glitter, glue, and ribbon.
2. **Decorate the Star**: Use glue and glitter to make the star shine. As you decorate, think about the qualities of kindness, courage, and wisdom that guided Finn on his journey.
3. **Add Your Light**: Once the star is decorated, hold it in your hands and make a wish or think of something kind you can do for someone this Christmas. This is your way of adding your light to the star.
4. **Hang the Star**: Place your Christmas Star on your tree, a symbol of the light you carry within you and the magic that shines brightest when shared with others.

Through Finn's journey to find the lost Christmas Star, we are reminded that the magic of Christmas lies in our hearts, waiting to be kindled and shared with the world. May your star shine brightly this holiday season!

Part 2: *Yuletide Traditions: Stories of Love and Giving*

Chapter 6: Gifts from the Heart

Christmas has always been more than the excitement of unwrapping gifts or the dazzling lights on the tree. At its core, the holiday embodies the spirit of giving, of small, thoughtful gestures that come from the heart. Gifts need not be grand or expensive; the most meaningful ones often carry a touch of love and sincerity, creating memories that linger long after the holiday season ends. This chapter brings together a collection of short stories that celebrate the joy of giving and the unexpected acts of kindness that reveal the true magic of Christmas.

1. The Woven Scarf

In a small, quiet village nestled among snowy hills, lived an elderly woman named Margaret. She was known for her kind heart and for knitting beautiful scarves, hats, and mittens for everyone in the village. She lived alone in a little cottage at the edge of the woods, her only companion a tabby cat named Whiskers. Margaret loved Christmas, not for the gifts she received, but for the joy of giving.

As Christmas approached, she decided to knit a special scarf, one that would be warmer than any she had ever made. She chose the finest wool, dyed in vibrant shades of red, green, and gold. As she wove the threads together, she thought about whom she would give this scarf to. She wanted it to go to someone who truly needed a touch of warmth and care this season.

One snowy evening, as Margaret walked through the village square, she noticed a boy sitting on a bench. His clothes were thin and worn, and he hugged his knees to keep warm. Margaret recognized him as Sam, the new child in town who had recently moved in with his aunt after his parents' passing. Her heart ached at the sight of him shivering in the cold.

Without hesitation, she approached him and draped the scarf around his shoulders. "Here, dear," she said with a warm smile. "A little something to keep you warm this winter."

Sam looked up, eyes wide with surprise and gratitude. "Thank you, ma'am," he whispered, his small fingers clutching the soft wool. It was the first time in weeks he had felt warmth—not just from the scarf, but from the unexpected kindness of a stranger.

As he walked home, Sam couldn't help but feel a little lighter, a little less alone. And Margaret, as she watched him go, felt her heart swell with joy. That night, the scarf seemed to glow softly in the moonlight, reflecting the love and warmth woven into every stitch.

2. The Snow Angel's Secret

In the bustling city, everyone seemed to be rushing about, buying gifts, and preparing for grand celebrations. Amidst the hurry and noise, a girl named Ella found herself feeling lost. Her family was going through a difficult time, and there wasn't enough money for Christmas presents this year. It wasn't the lack of gifts that saddened Ella, but the thought that they might not be able to share the joy of the holiday with others as they usually did.

One evening, as she walked through the city park, she noticed something peculiar. Nestled beneath a snow-covered tree was a little angel figurine, its wings dusted with frost and a golden halo glistening in the dim light. Ella picked it up carefully, marveling at its delicate beauty.

Clutched in the angel's hand was a tiny scroll of paper. Unrolling it, Ella read the message: "Give this angel to someone who needs joy. By giving, you will receive more than you could ever imagine."

Ella pondered the note's meaning as she carried the angel home. The next day, she noticed her elderly neighbor, Mrs. Thornton, sitting alone on her porch. Mrs. Thornton's husband had passed away earlier that year, and she rarely left the house anymore. Ella suddenly knew what she had to do.

She wrapped the angel in a bit of cloth, adding a sprig of holly for decoration, and brought it over to Mrs. Thornton's house. "I found this angel," Ella said, handing over the gift. "I thought you might like it."

Mrs. Thornton's eyes filled with tears as she took the angel. "Thank you, dear," she said softly, her voice trembling. "It's been a hard year, and this is the first Christmas decoration I have put up. It means more to me than you know."

As Ella walked back home, she felt a warmth spreading through her chest. In giving away the angel, she had found something far more valuable—joy. The next day, she woke up to find a small package on her doorstep. Inside was a handmade ornament, carved from wood, with a note: "To the girl who brings light to others, may your heart always be full."

3. The Bakery's Gift

Mr. Hill ran the only bakery in the village of Pine Hollow. It was a cozy, inviting place where the scent of freshly baked bread, pies, and cookies filled the air. Every Christmas, Mr. Hill gave away loaves of bread to those who couldn't afford to buy their own, earning him the love and gratitude of the townspeople.

One Christmas Eve, as Mr. Hill was about to close up shop, a young woman walked in, carrying a baby bundled in a blanket. She looked tired and cold. "Do you have any bread left, sir?" she asked hesitantly, her voice wavering.

Mr. Hill glanced around. The shelves were nearly bare, as he had given away most of his goods already. But there, in the corner, was a loaf of his finest spiced bread—the one he had baked for his own Christmas dinner.

Without a second thought, he picked up the loaf, wrapped it carefully in brown paper, and handed it to her. "Here, take this," he said warmly. "Merry Christmas."

Tears welled up in the woman's eyes as she took the bread. "Thank you," she whispered. "You don't know how much this means to me and my baby."

As she left, Mr. Hill felt a pang of worry—what would he serve for his own dinner now? But as he turned to clean up, he noticed something on the counter. There, resting where the loaf had been, was a small silver coin, old and tarnished but shining brightly in the light of the bakery.

That night, when Mr. Hill went to fetch water from the well, he found it covered in the most beautiful frost patterns. And at the very bottom of the well lay a basket, filled with fresh bread, cakes, and fruits. A note was tucked inside: "To the one who gives without asking, here is the joy you deserve."

4. The Unexpected Visitor

Deep in the woods lived a carpenter named Thomas. He was known for his skill in making wooden toys, which he would sell at the market. Christmas was his busiest time of year, and he worked late into the nights, carving toy soldiers, rocking horses, and dollhouses. However, this year, he felt a deep sadness. His wife had passed away in the spring, and he found little joy in his work.

One cold afternoon, as Thomas was finishing up a batch of toys, there was a knock on his door. He opened it to find a young girl standing there, her cheeks flushed with cold and her eyes wide with wonder. "Hello," she said shyly. "My name is Lily. I live in the village nearby. I heard you make the best toys."

Thomas managed a small smile. "I do my best," he replied, glancing at the toys scattered around his workshop.

Lily looked at them longingly. "I don't have money to buy a toy," she admitted. "But I thought I'd come see them, because looking at beautiful things makes me happy."

Thomas's heart softened. "Wait here," he said, walking to his workbench. He picked up a small wooden horse, painted with bright colors, and handed it to her. "Here, take this. It's a gift."

Lily's eyes lit up. "Really? For me?" She hugged the toy to her chest, her smile lighting up the room.

"Yes," Thomas said, feeling a warmth he hadn't felt in months. "Merry Christmas, Lily."

After she left, Thomas sat down by the fire, staring at the flames. For the first time in a long while, he felt a spark of happiness. He realized that the act of giving, of making someone else smile, had rekindled the joy in his heart.

The next morning, Thomas woke up to find his workshop filled with light. Sunbeams streamed through the windows, casting a golden glow on the wooden toys. He walked to his workbench and found, to his surprise, that the toy soldiers he had left unfinished were now complete. Each one stood proudly, as if they had been touched by magic. In that moment, Thomas knew that the spirit of Christmas had visited his home, reminding him that giving from the heart could bring light even to the darkest of times.

Reflection on the Gifts from the Heart

These stories remind us that Christmas gifts are more than just objects wrapped in paper. They are expressions of love, kindness, and the desire to bring joy to others. The most meaningful gifts often come from unexpected places, created not with wealth but with sincerity and thoughtfulness. The act of giving, whether big or small, has the power to warm hearts, brighten spirits, and weave the magic of Christmas into our lives.

Activity: Creating a Gift from the Heart

Inspired by the stories of kindness, try making a simple, heartfelt gift to give this Christmas. Here's an idea:

- **Warmth in a Jar**: Fill a glass jar with hot cocoa mix, marshmallows, and a candy cane. Attach a small tag with a message, such as "A little warmth for a cold winter's day." This small gesture is easy to make but carries the warmth and thoughtfulness of a gift from the heart.
- **Handwritten Letter**: Sometimes, words are the most precious gifts we can give. Write a heartfelt letter to a friend, family member, or neighbor, expressing your gratitude for their presence in your life.

Christmas is the season of giving, not just in material form, but in the moments we share, the kindness we show, and the joy we spread. May these stories inspire you to find the magic of giving from the heart, creating memories that will last for many Christmases to come.

Chapter 7: The Christmas Market

The Christmas market is a celebration that has stood the test of time, dating back centuries as a cherished tradition that fills towns and cities with joy, warmth, and a sense of community. From the cobblestone streets of European villages to the bustling squares of modern cities, Christmas markets have long been the heart of holiday festivities, offering a blend of sights, scents, and sounds that capture the spirit of the season. In this chapter, we'll delve into the history of Christmas markets and transport ourselves into a fictional story set in an old village, where the magic of the market changes lives.

The History of Christmas Markets

The tradition of Christmas markets dates back to the late Middle Ages in German-speaking parts of Europe. The first known market was the "December Market" in Vienna, which took place in 1298, though it wasn't until the 14th and 15th centuries that the markets became widespread across Germany. One of the oldest recorded Christmas markets is the Dresden Striezelmarkt, which began in 1434. These markets started as one-day fairs, allowing townspeople to stock up on supplies for the winter and purchase special items for the Christmas feast.

As the centuries passed, Christmas markets grew from simple gatherings into elaborate festivities, filled with vendors selling everything from handmade crafts to sweet treats. Wooden stalls adorned with pine boughs and twinkling lights became a hallmark of these markets, where visitors could purchase baked goods, mulled wine, candles, and toys. The markets became places not just for shopping, but for experiencing the joy of the season. Carolers sang traditional Christmas songs, while the air filled with the scents of roasting chestnuts, gingerbread, and spiced cider.

In many regions, markets also included a Nativity scene, bringing to life the story of Christmas. Children would gather to see Saint Nicholas or Father Christmas as he made his way through the market, sharing small gifts and treats. Even today, Christmas markets continue to be a beloved tradition, enchanting visitors with their festive atmosphere and the sense of nostalgia they evoke.

A Story from the Village Market: The Miracle of Silverwood

In the quaint village of Silverwood, nestled deep within a valley and surrounded by snow-capped mountains, the annual Christmas market was the most anticipated event of the year. For centuries, the market had been a place where villagers gathered to celebrate the season, share their handmade wares, and rekindle the sense of community that thrived in winter's embrace.

It was said that Silverwood's market was blessed by the spirit of Christmas itself, for each year something miraculous happened within its bustling streets. Some years it was a sudden snowfall that covered the market in a blanket of glittering white, while in others, the stars above shone so brightly that it seemed the whole sky was singing. But there was one year, many winters ago, when the market witnessed a miracle that would be remembered forever.

The Village's Hope

It was the winter of 1872, and the village of Silverwood had fallen on hard times. A harsh storm had struck the valley in early November, leaving many homes damaged and food supplies scarce. Despite the hardship, the villagers worked tirelessly to prepare for the Christmas market, believing that its magic might bring some cheer to their troubled hearts.

Among the villagers was a young woman named Clara, who had recently lost her parents and now struggled to care for her little brother, Tobias. Clara was a talented weaver, known for her beautiful scarves and blankets, which she crafted from the softest wool. However, this year, she barely had enough material to make more than a handful of items. Despite this, she decided to set up a small stall at the market, hoping that a few sales might help her earn enough to buy the food and firewood they desperately needed for the winter.

The market day arrived, and the village square transformed into a scene of festivity. Wooden stalls, draped with garlands of holly and mistletoe, lined the cobblestone paths. Lanterns hung from the trees, casting a warm, golden light over the snow-covered ground. Vendors filled their booths with baked goods, candles, toys, and handcrafted ornaments, while the smell of roasted chestnuts and mulled cider wafted through the air.

Clara's stall was modest, adorned with only a few scarves and a blanket. As she watched the villagers and travelers bustle about, she couldn't help but feel a pang of worry. What if no one bought her wares? How would she and Tobias make it through the winter?

The Old Man's Gift

As the market grew busier, an old man in a long, tattered coat approached Clara's stall. His face was weathered, and his eyes shone with a kindness that took her by surprise.

"Good evening, dear," he greeted with a warm smile. "You have woven these scarves beautifully."

Clara blushed slightly and nodded. "Thank you, sir. They are made from the last of my wool," she admitted, her voice tinged with the weight of her worries.

The old man picked up a scarf, running his fingers over the intricate patterns. "How much for this one?" he asked.

"Five silver pieces," Clara replied, though she knew it was more than most could afford. She braced herself for his rejection.

The old man reached into his coat pocket and pulled out a small pouch. To Clara's astonishment, he handed her not five, but ten silver pieces.

"Here, take this," he said kindly, placing the scarf in his coat. "And use the extra to keep you warm this winter."

Clara's eyes widened. "Oh, sir, I... I cannot accept this," she stammered. "It's too much."

"Nonsense," the man chuckled. "It's a gift from the heart, for you and your brother." And before Clara could protest further, he turned and disappeared into the crowd.

The Spirit of Giving

As the evening progressed, Clara sold a few more scarves, but the warmth from the old man's unexpected generosity stayed with her. She used the silver he had given her to buy food and firewood for the coming weeks. But the next morning, when she awoke and looked at her small pouch of coins, she found something incredible.

The pouch was filled to the brim with silver pieces, far more than what she had received at the market. Bewildered, Clara counted the coins over and over, but the amount never changed. It was more than enough to last her and Tobias through the winter, and then some.

Word of the miracle spread quickly through the village, and soon everyone was talking about the old man who had visited Clara's stall. Some said he was a spirit sent by Saint Nicholas, others believed he was one of the wise men who wandered the world during Christmas, spreading joy to those in need. Whatever the truth, the villagers came together, sharing what they had, inspired by the old man's act of kindness.

In the days that followed, the market continued to be filled with the spirit of giving. People bought gifts for one another, not out of obligation, but out of a genuine desire to share joy. The bakers gave away loaves of bread to those who couldn't afford them. The toymakers crafted extra toys to be left at the doorsteps of families with children. Even the candle-maker, who had been struggling to keep her business afloat, lit up the entire market with lanterns, filling the night with a soft, comforting glow.

The Market's Blessing

The village of Silverwood experienced a Christmas unlike any other. Despite the harsh winter and the challenges they faced, the market had brought warmth and light into every heart. And from that year on, the villagers made a vow to always keep the spirit of giving alive during the Christmas market.

Each year, an extra stall was set up at the market, filled with gifts that anyone could take for free. It became known as the "Gift from the Heart" stall, a reminder of the old man's kindness and the magic that happens when people come together to help one another.

Clara, now an elderly woman herself, continued to sell her scarves at the market, but she never forgot that winter when a simple act of generosity had changed her life. She often told the story to the children of the village, ending it with a smile and a twinkle in her eye. "You see, my dears," she would say, "the market is more than a place to buy things. It is a place where the magic of Christmas lives in each act of kindness, big or small. And that magic, once given, always finds its way back to you."

Activity: Creating Your Own Market Magic

To capture a bit of the joy and magic of the Christmas market, try creating your own "Gift from the Heart" for someone in need this season.

1. **Warm Winter Packs**: Put together small care packages with warm items like gloves, scarves, socks, and a packet of hot cocoa. Give them to those in your community who might need extra warmth this winter.

2. **Christmas Market at Home**: Set up a little market at home or in your neighborhood where people can exchange small handmade gifts, like cookies, candles, or ornaments. It's a wonderful way to foster the spirit of giving and community, just like in Silverwood.

A Legacy of Giving

The story of the Christmas market in Silverwood reminds us that the true beauty of the season is found not in what we receive, but in what we give. Whether it's a simple scarf, a loaf of bread, or a warm smile, every act of kindness adds a bit of magic to the world. And just like the old man in the story, we can be the spark that lights up someone else's Christmas, transforming the market—and our hearts—into a place where the spirit of giving lives on forever.

Chapter 8: St. Nicholas' Day

St. Nicholas' Day, celebrated on December 6th, is a day that brings warmth, kindness, and a bit of magic to the Christmas season. This day is dedicated to the legend of St. Nicholas, a 4th-century bishop known for his generosity and secret gift-giving. It is from his legacy that the beloved figure of Santa Claus, or Father Christmas, has evolved across cultures. In this chapter, we will explore the origins of St. Nicholas, how his story shaped the modern Santa Claus, and the unique ways different countries celebrate this day, showcasing the rich and varied traditions that have grown around this ancient figure.

The Origins of St. Nicholas

St. Nicholas was born around 280 AD in the village of Patara, which was part of modern-day Turkey. From a young age, he was known for his piety and generosity. Orphaned at an early age, he inherited a significant amount of wealth from his parents. Rather than spending it on himself, Nicholas chose to use his fortune to help the poor, the sick, and those in need. He became known as a secret benefactor, often leaving gifts for people under the cover of night to avoid attention.

One of the most famous legends of St. Nicholas tells of a poor man with three daughters. In those days, a woman needed a dowry—a sum of money and goods—to be eligible for marriage. Without dowries, the daughters would likely be sold into servitude. Hearing of the family's plight, Nicholas decided to help. Under the cover of darkness, he secretly dropped a bag of gold coins through their window. The gold provided enough dowry for the eldest daughter to marry. Nicholas did the same for the second daughter, and when the poor man lay in wait to discover his mysterious benefactor, Nicholas revealed himself, urging the man to keep his identity a secret.

This act of kindness became the foundation of St. Nicholas' reputation as a protector of the poor and a bringer of gifts, especially to children. As the bishop of Myra, St. Nicholas became known for his compassion and miracles, and after his death on December 6th, he was venerated as a saint. Over the centuries, stories of his deeds spread throughout Europe, and his feast day became a time for giving and charity, particularly towards children.

The Evolution into Santa Claus

As the legend of St. Nicholas spread across Europe, he began to take on different characteristics based on regional folklore and customs. During the Protestant Reformation in the 16th century, the veneration of saints, including St. Nicholas, was discouraged in many parts of Europe. However, his legend lived on, transforming into various gift-bringing figures that we recognize today.

In the Netherlands, he became known as *Sinterklaas*, a white-bearded man dressed in a red bishop's robe who arrives on a ship from Spain to deliver gifts to children on the eve of December 6th. The Dutch settlers brought the tradition of Sinterklaas to America in the 17th century, where his name evolved into "Santa Claus." Over time, the image of Santa Claus was further shaped by literature, art, and popular culture, becoming the jolly, rotund figure in a red suit who delivers presents on Christmas Eve.

Meanwhile, other countries adapted the figure of St. Nicholas to fit their own traditions. In Germany, he became known as *Weihnachtsmann* (the Christmas Man), while in England, he merged with the figure of Father Christmas. In France, he is celebrated as *Père Noël*, and in Italy, as *Babbo Natale*. Despite these regional variations, the essence of St. Nicholas' generosity and gift-giving remains at the heart of each tradition.

Celebrating St. Nicholas' Day Around the World

St. Nicholas' Day is still widely celebrated in many countries, each with its own unique customs that capture the spirit of giving, kindness, and joy. Here are some of the ways different cultures honor St. Nicholas:

1. The Netherlands: Sinterklaas and Zwarte Piet

In the Netherlands, the celebration of St. Nicholas, or *Sinterklaas*, is a grand affair that begins weeks before December 6th. Sinterklaas is depicted as an elderly man with a long white beard, wearing a red bishop's robe and a mitre. He arrives by steamboat from Spain, accompanied by his helpers, known as *Zwarte Piet* (Black Pete). The arrival, called *intocht*, is a much-anticipated event that involves parades, music, and festivities.

On the evening of December 5th, known as *Sinterklaasavond* or *Pakjesavond* (Present Evening), children place their shoes by the fireplace or the door, along with a carrot or hay for Sinterklaas' horse. They sing songs and go to bed, hoping to find their shoes filled with treats, small gifts, and sweets by morning. Traditional gifts include chocolate letters, marzipan figures, and small toys, along with personalized poems that offer a humorous reflection on the recipient's year.

2. Germany: Nikolaustag

In Germany, St. Nicholas' Day, known as *Nikolaustag*, is celebrated on December 6th. On the evening of December 5th, children polish their shoes and leave them outside their doors, hoping that *Nikolaus* will fill them with treats like nuts, oranges, chocolate, and small toys. Sometimes, St. Nicholas is accompanied by *Knecht Ruprecht* or *Krampus*, a darker figure who carries a sack of coal and warns children to be good.

Unlike Santa Claus, who comes on Christmas Eve, Nikolaus focuses on small gifts and treats, with the main gift-giving taking place on Christmas. The tradition of *Nikolaustag* encourages children to be kind and generous, reflecting the values St. Nicholas embodied.

3. France: Saint Nicolas and Père Fouettard

In parts of France, particularly in the region of Lorraine, St. Nicholas' Day is a cherished holiday. Children leave their shoes out by the fireplace on the evening of December 5th, and St. Nicholas fills them with candy, fruit, and small gifts. However, he is often accompanied by *Père Fouettard* (Father Whipper), a figure who carries a birch rod to remind children to behave.

In the town of Nancy, a grand procession is held in honor of St. Nicholas, featuring a parade, music, and a fireworks display. This tradition celebrates both the generosity of St. Nicholas and the importance of good behavior throughout the year.

4. Italy: San Nicola and La Befana

In Italy, particularly in the regions of Bari and Sicily, St. Nicholas is known as *San Nicola*, and his feast day is celebrated with parades, processions, and special masses. In Bari, where St. Nicholas' relics are housed, the *Festa di San Nicola* includes a reenactment of his arrival by sea, symbolizing his role as the protector of sailors and children.

While St. Nicholas' Day marks the beginning of the Christmas season, the Italian tradition extends to *La Befana*, the kind, witch-like figure who brings gifts on Epiphany (January 6th). It is believed that Befana was searching for the Christ child, guided by the Three Wise Men, and now brings gifts to children in his honor.

5. Russia and Eastern Europe: Ded Moroz and Svyatki

In Russia and Eastern Europe, the figure of St. Nicholas has influenced the development of *Ded Moroz* (Grandfather Frost), who brings gifts to children on New Year's Eve. However, St. Nicholas' Day is still observed, particularly among Orthodox Christians. In Ukraine, for example, children place their shoes by the windowsill, hoping that St. Nicholas will leave small gifts if they have been good.

In Poland, *Mikołajki* is celebrated on December 6th, when children wake up to find small presents or sweets under their pillows. The tradition emphasizes the importance of kindness, generosity, and the magic that St. Nicholas brings to the Christmas season.

The True Spirit of St. Nicholas

St. Nicholas' Day, in all its forms, reminds us of the importance of giving without expecting anything in return. The story of St. Nicholas embodies the spirit of generosity, compassion, and secret acts of kindness. As his legend evolved into the modern-day Santa Claus, the values he represented—caring for others, spreading joy, and sharing what we have—remained at the heart of Christmas.

While the figure of Santa Claus has become a symbol of Christmas gift-giving, the origins of this tradition lie in the simple yet profound deeds of a man who quietly helped those in need. Through the global variations of St. Nicholas, we see a reflection of humanity's collective desire to make the world a warmer, more compassionate place, especially during the darkest days of winter.

Activity: Celebrating St. Nicholas' Day at Home

Celebrate St. Nicholas' Day with an activity that captures the spirit of kindness and giving:

St. Nicholas' Shoe Surprise:

1. On the evening of December 5th, gather a pair of shoes and place them by the front door or the fireplace.
2. Fill them with small treats, such as chocolate coins, fruit, nuts, and perhaps a small toy or a handwritten note of encouragement.
3. For added fun, encourage children to polish their shoes beforehand, just as children do in Germany and the Netherlands.
4. As you fill the shoes, take a moment to reflect on the story of St. Nicholas and think of ways to spread kindness to those around you.

By incorporating this tradition into your holiday celebrations, you keep the legend of St. Nicholas alive, sharing his message of generosity and warmth with the next generation. Just as St. Nicholas' acts of kindness inspired stories and traditions around the world, so too can we bring joy to others through simple, heartfelt gestures.

Chapter 9: The Evergreen's Tale

Christmas wreaths and garlands, with their lush greenery, glistening berries, and fragrant pinecones, are some of the most cherished symbols of the holiday season. They adorn our homes, hang on our doors, and wrap around staircases and fireplaces, bringing a touch of nature's winter beauty indoors. But beyond their decorative charm lies a rich history steeped in magical lore and ancient traditions. In this chapter, we will explore the origins of the Christmas wreath and garlands, uncovering the myths and legends that make these evergreens so enchanting.

The Ancient Symbolism of Evergreens

Long before the Christmas wreath became a hallmark of holiday décor, evergreens held deep spiritual and symbolic meaning in various cultures around the world. In ancient times, people revered evergreen trees, such as pine, fir, spruce, and holly, for their ability to remain vibrant and green even during the harshest winters. This resilience was seen as a representation of life, renewal, and protection against the forces of darkness.

In many pagan cultures, the winter solstice—occurring around December 21st—was a time of great significance. It marked the longest night of the year and the gradual return of the sun's light. To celebrate the rebirth of the sun and the hope of spring, ancient peoples brought evergreens into their homes, believing that these plants held magical properties. They created wreaths, garlands, and other decorations to honor nature's endurance and to invite prosperity, health, and protection for the coming year.

The circular shape of the wreath itself carried powerful symbolism. Circles, with no beginning or end, represented eternity, unity, and the cyclical nature of life. For the ancient Romans, wreaths made from laurel leaves were symbols of victory and honor, often worn by leaders and athletes. As these traditions evolved, the evergreen wreath became a symbol not just of nature's strength, but also of hope, faith, and the continuity of life.

The Magical Lore of the Wreath

In northern European folklore, it was believed that evergreen plants possessed mystical qualities that could ward off evil spirits and misfortune. One legend tells of the *Evergreen's Blessing*, a tale passed down through generations about the magical properties of the wreath.

According to this legend, during the darkest days of winter, when the world was cold and covered in snow, the forest spirits gathered to protect the woods. They chose the evergreens—pines, firs, and hollies—to be their guardians. As a token of their blessing, the spirits infused the leaves and branches of these trees with magic, ensuring they would remain green and alive throughout the season. To harness this protective magic, the forest spirits taught humans to weave the branches into wreaths and garlands.

It was said that a wreath hung on the door of a home would create a magical barrier, keeping out ill fortune and inviting good spirits to enter. The circular shape of the wreath acted as a symbol of unity and harmony, drawing in the warmth of friendship and family. The berries and pinecones often added to wreaths were considered tokens of abundance, promising a fruitful year ahead.

Another story speaks of the *Wreath of Light*, a magical wreath that would glow softly in the dark. It was said that this wreath was created by the forest spirits themselves to guide lost travelers through the woods on winter nights. Those who stumbled upon the Wreath of Light found their way safely home, and many began the tradition of placing wreaths on their doors as a beacon of welcome and hope during the long, cold nights of winter.

The Christmas Wreath and Christian Tradition

As Christianity spread across Europe, many of the existing pagan customs and symbols, including those associated with evergreens, were incorporated into Christian practices. The wreath took on new meaning as a symbol of Christ's eternal love and the promise of everlasting life. The circular form of the wreath came to represent God's infinite love, while the evergreens used in its creation symbolized the hope and renewal found in Christ's birth.

In the 16th century, the tradition of the *Advent wreath* began in Germany. Made from evergreen branches and adorned with four candles—each representing a Sunday leading up to Christmas—this wreath became a focal point for reflection, prayer, and anticipation of Christ's coming. As each candle was lit, it marked the progression towards the celebration of the light that entered the world with the birth of Jesus.

The use of holly in wreaths also took on Christian symbolism. The sharp leaves of the holly were said to represent the crown of thorns worn by Jesus during his crucifixion, while the red berries symbolized his blood. Thus, the wreath became a powerful reminder of both Christ's sacrifice and the hope of redemption.

The Story of the Yule Garland

In Scandinavian and Celtic traditions, the *Yule garland* was an important part of the winter solstice celebrations. The word "Yule" itself is rooted in ancient Nordic traditions, referring to the festival marking the rebirth of the sun. As part of the Yule festivities, people would decorate their homes with garlands made from pine, spruce, and ivy, often draping them over doorways, hearths, and windows.

One legend from Celtic folklore tells of a magical garland woven by the forest queen, a mystical figure who reigned over the winter woods. It was said that this garland held the essence of the forest's vitality, woven from the oldest and wisest trees. According to the tale, the forest queen would hang the garland on the highest branch of an ancient oak each year during the winter solstice. From this spot, the garland's magic would radiate, renewing the strength of the woods and ensuring that life would return with the spring.

To honor the forest queen and partake in her magic, villagers began making their own Yule garlands to hang in their homes. They believed that the garland would bring protection, health, and good fortune throughout the winter months. The garlands were often adorned with dried fruits, nuts, and ribbons, each element carrying its own symbolism of prosperity, fertility, and joy.

The Modern Christmas Wreath and Garland

Today, Christmas wreaths and garlands continue to be a beloved part of holiday traditions around the world. While their magical origins may have faded into legend, their beauty and symbolism remain. Modern wreaths are often embellished with a variety of decorations—ornaments, bells, ribbons, and candles—each adding to the festive spirit.

In some cultures, the act of creating a wreath or garland is itself a cherished tradition. Families gather to weave evergreen branches together, adding personal touches such as handmade bows or favorite trinkets. The wreaths are then hung on front doors, windows, and walls, serving as a welcome to guests and a reminder of the enduring warmth of the season.

For many, the wreath also serves as a symbol of hope. In times of hardship or uncertainty, its circle of green offers a reminder that life continues in cycles, and that light and joy can always be found, even in the darkest days of winter.

A Story from the Evergreen's Tale: The Wreathmaker's Blessing

In a small mountain village, there lived a wreathmaker named Liora. She was known far and wide for her beautiful wreaths, which she crafted from the freshest evergreens gathered from the forest each winter. Liora believed that each wreath carried a bit of the forest's magic and that by giving them to others, she was sharing that magic.

As Christmas approached one particularly harsh winter, the village was gripped by worry. The snow had fallen heavily, isolating them from the neighboring towns, and food supplies were running low. Despite the difficulties, Liora continued to weave her wreaths, determined to spread a bit of hope and cheer.

One evening, as she gathered pine branches in the forest, she came upon an ancient tree, its bark covered in frost. Beneath its branches lay a small, shimmering object—a sprig of holly with the brightest red berries she had ever seen. Liora picked it up and felt a warmth spread through her hands. "It is the forest's blessing," she whispered, realizing that this holly was a gift from the forest spirits.

Liora hurried back to her workshop and began crafting a wreath using the holly sprig. She wove it with care, adding pinecones, berries, and ribbons. As she worked, she whispered a wish into the wreath—a wish for warmth, abundance, and unity for her village.

On Christmas Eve, Liora hung the wreath on the door of the village's gathering hall. That night, as the villagers came together, they felt a sudden change. The cold seemed less biting, and the air filled with a fragrance of pine and warmth. To their astonishment, they found that the wreath was glowing softly, casting a gentle light across the hall.

The villagers gathered around, feeling the warmth of the wreath's magic. It was as if the forest itself had blessed them, renewing their spirits. In the days that followed, the snow began to thaw, revealing paths to the neighboring towns. Supplies arrived, and the village made it through the winter, united by the wreath's blessing.

From that year on, Liora's wreaths became a cherished part of the village's Christmas tradition. Each family would hang a wreath on their door, believing that it carried the same blessing—the gift of light, warmth, and hope.

Activity: Making Your Own Wreath or Garland

To bring the magic of the evergreens into your home, create your own Christmas wreath or garland using natural materials. Here's how to make a simple wreath that carries the symbolism of hope, unity, and protection:

1. **Gather Materials:** Fresh evergreen branches (pine, fir, cedar, or holly), floral wire, wire wreath frame or a circle made from flexible branches, decorative elements like pinecones, berries, ribbons, and candles.

2. **Weave the Wreath:** Start by attaching small bundles of evergreen branches to the wreath frame using floral wire. Layer the branches in the same direction to create a lush, full look. Add pinecones, berries, and any other decorative items as you weave.

3. **Add a Symbol of Light:** Incorporate a candle or a small string of battery-operated lights into your wreath. This symbolizes the light of hope that the wreath brings into your home.

4. **Hang the Wreath:** Place your wreath on your door, in a window, or over your fireplace as a reminder of the strength and unity that evergreens represent.

5. **Create a Garland:** For a garland, use a long piece of sturdy twine or ribbon. Attach evergreen branches, pinecones, and berries along the length, securing them with wire. Drape the garland over doorways, staircases, or mantels to bring the forest's magic indoors.

As you create your wreath or garland, take a moment to reflect on its symbolism. Like the evergreens that remain vibrant through the winter, may your wreath be a reminder of hope, strength, and the magic that lives in every corner of the season.

The evergreen's tale, woven through centuries of tradition and folklore, continues to bring warmth to our homes during the coldest days of the year. In each wreath and garland, we carry a piece of nature's resilience, a circle of life and light that welcomes all who pass through our doors.

Chapter 10: Yuletide Spirits

When we think of Christmas, it often conjures up images of warmth, joy, twinkling lights, and laughter. Yet, woven into the fabric of Christmas lore are tales of spirits that walk the earth during this magical time of year. Some of these spirits are benevolent, bringing blessings and joy to those they encounter. Others are eerie and ominous, serving as cautionary figures that remind us of the balance between light and dark, generosity and greed. In this chapter, we explore the vast and fascinating world of Yuletide spirits, from the merry ghosts who spread cheer to the more haunting figures who roam the winter nights.

The Origins of Yuletide Spirits

The idea of ghosts and spirits visiting during the Christmas season is rooted in ancient winter solstice celebrations. The winter solstice, falling around December 21st, marks the longest night of the year and has been observed for millennia as a time when the veil between the worlds is thin. In Norse mythology, the *Wild Hunt* was said to take place during the solstice, with Odin leading a host of spirits across the sky, a harbinger of changes to come. Many cultures believed that during this time, the spirits of the dead could return to the world of the living, bringing messages, blessings, or warnings.

As these solstice traditions merged with Christian practices, the lore of Yuletide spirits continued to evolve. By the Middle Ages, the concept of Christmas ghosts had become a popular element of the season, especially in England and other parts of Europe. These tales were often cautionary, reminding people to be kind, generous, and mindful of their actions during the season of goodwill. In Victorian England, the tradition of telling ghost stories on Christmas Eve became particularly fashionable, a custom that was famously immortalized in Charles Dickens' "A Christmas Carol."

The Spirits of Christmas: From the Joyous to the Eerie

The Yuletide season is home to a variety of spirits, each with its own unique character and purpose. Some are merry and kind, embodying the joy of the season, while others are haunting and stern, serving as reminders of moral and spiritual truths. Here, we explore some of the most intriguing spirits that have become part of Christmas lore.

1. The Spirits of Christmas Past, Present, and Future

Perhaps the most well-known Christmas spirits are those from Dickens' classic tale, *A Christmas Carol.* In this story, the miserly Ebenezer Scrooge is visited by three spirits on Christmas Eve. These ghosts, each representing different aspects of Christmas, serve to teach Scrooge the value of kindness, generosity, and the fleeting nature of time.

- **The Ghost of Christmas Past**: This spirit often appears as a shimmering figure, glowing with a soft, ethereal light. It represents nostalgia and the innocence of childhood, reminding us of the memories and experiences that shape who we are. The Ghost of Christmas Past is both comforting and bittersweet, showing Scrooge glimpses of his younger years and the choices that led to his present loneliness.

- **The Ghost of Christmas Present**: Usually depicted as a jolly, larger-than-life figure draped in green robes, the Ghost of Christmas Present embodies the warmth, generosity, and joy of the season. This spirit reveals the lives of others during Christmas, highlighting both the blessings and hardships experienced by people around us. It serves as a reminder to be grateful and compassionate in the here and now.

- **The Ghost of Christmas Yet to Come (Future)**: The most ominous of the three, this spirit is often shown as a dark, hooded figure, silent and foreboding. It represents the unknown future, warning us of the consequences of our actions and the importance of change. By showing Scrooge a grim future shaped by his selfishness, this spirit ultimately guides him toward redemption.

These spirits, though fictional, embody powerful themes of reflection, empathy, and transformation. They have become iconic symbols of the Christmas season, reminding us to cherish the past, embrace the present, and strive for a better future.

2. The Christmas Brownies and Household Spirits

In the folklore of Scotland and northern England, *brownies* are small, helpful household spirits who come out at night to assist with chores. During the Christmas season, brownies are believed to be particularly active, bringing tidings of joy to the homes they visit. Families would leave out small offerings, such as milk, honey, or bread, to thank the brownies for their unseen help.

These household spirits are friendly and protective but can be easily offended. If mistreated or neglected, a brownie might become a *boggart*—a mischievous, sometimes troublesome spirit that plays pranks and creates chaos. This dual nature of the brownies serves as a reminder to treat others, seen and unseen, with kindness and respect, especially during the holiday season.

In German folklore, there are similar household spirits known as *kobolds* or *house gnomes.* During Yuletide, these spirits are said to bring good fortune to well-kept homes. To invite their blessings, families would sweep the hearth and prepare a special dish of porridge or sweet cakes for the household spirits to enjoy.

3. The Tomte and Nisse of Scandinavia

In Scandinavian countries, the *tomte* (Sweden) or *nisse* (Norway and Denmark) is a small, gnome-like spirit that watches over farms and homes, particularly during the winter months. With their long beards and pointed hats, these spirits are thought to bring good luck and protection, provided they are treated with respect.

During Christmas, the tomte or nisse becomes a central figure of folklore. It is customary for families to leave out a bowl of porridge with butter on Christmas Eve as an offering to these spirits. If neglected or angered, however, the tomte might play tricks or bring misfortune to the household. This tradition serves as a reminder of the importance of generosity and gratitude, values that are at the heart of the Christmas season.

In modern times, the tomte or nisse has become associated with the Christmas gift-bringer, similar to Santa Claus. Children eagerly await the arrival of the tomte on Christmas Eve, hoping for small gifts left under the tree or in stockings.

4. The Wild Hunt and the Winter Ghosts

One of the more eerie aspects of Yuletide lore is the legend of the *Wild Hunt*. Originating in Norse and Germanic mythology, the Wild Hunt is a ghostly procession of spirits and supernatural beings, led by a powerful figure such as Odin or a mythic hunter. During the winter solstice, it was believed that the Wild Hunt rode through the skies, a portent of changes and omens for the coming year.

People in medieval Europe were cautious during the nights of the solstice, wary of encountering the spectral hunt. To protect their homes, they would hang garlands of holly and place candles in windows to ward off wandering spirits. Some legends even speak of the *Yule Cat* and *Yule Goat*—beings that traveled with the hunt, visiting homes and assessing whether the inhabitants had been industrious and prepared for the winter.

While the Wild Hunt may sound frightening, its lore carries a deeper meaning. It serves as a reminder of the cycle of nature and the transformative power of the winter season. The hunt represents the forces of change and the need to honor the natural world's rhythms, even those that seem dark or foreboding.

5. The Benevolent Spirits of St. Nicholas' Night

On December 5th, the eve of St. Nicholas' Day, many European countries celebrate the arrival of *St. Nicholas* accompanied by a host of spirits, ranging from angelic to mischievous. In some regions, St. Nicholas is joined by a devilish figure, *Krampus* or *Knecht Ruprecht*, who serves as a foil to the benevolent saint. While St. Nicholas rewards good children with gifts and sweets, Krampus carries a bundle of birch rods, reminding children to be on their best behavior.

Despite his frightening appearance, Krampus is not purely malevolent. Instead, he represents the balance between reward and consequence, joy and discipline. The presence of such spirits during the Christmas season underscores the importance of kindness, humility, and the awareness that our actions have both immediate and lasting effects.

Yuletide Spirits Today: From Legends to Traditions

While many of these Yuletide spirits originate from ancient legends and folklore, their influence is still felt in modern Christmas traditions. The telling of ghost stories on Christmas Eve, popularized in Victorian England, has become part of the holiday's cultural tapestry. Charles Dickens' "A Christmas Carol" remains a poignant reminder of the transformative power of Christmas and the importance of compassion, generosity, and reflection.

In many households, the custom of leaving out food offerings—whether for Santa Claus, the tomte, or other spirits—reflects an enduring desire to honor the spirit of giving and to invite blessings into our homes. The lore of Yuletide spirits serves to remind us that Christmas is a time of wonder, filled with both light and shadows, joy and introspection.

Activity: Creating a Yuletide Spirit Offering

To connect with the magic of Yuletide spirits, consider making a small offering in honor of the household spirits, such as the tomte, brownies, or even the benevolent spirits of St. Nicholas. Here's how to create a simple Yuletide offering:

1. **Select Your Offering:** Traditional offerings include a bowl of porridge with a dab of butter, cookies, milk, or a piece of fruit. You can also prepare a small plate with bread, nuts, or sweets.
2. **Create a Welcoming Space:** Choose a spot near the hearth, doorway, or a cozy nook to place your offering. Add a candle or a small evergreen branch to symbolize warmth and welcome.
3. **Leave a Message:** Write a short note expressing your gratitude for the blessings of the season and your hope for goodwill and protection. Place the note with the offering.
4. **Reflect on the Season:** As you leave your offering, take a moment to reflect on the stories of Yuletide spirits and the values they represent—generosity, kindness, protection, and the beauty of transformation.

By honoring these ancient traditions, you bring a touch of the season's magic into your home. Whether you believe in the literal presence of spirits or simply wish to celebrate the folklore, these small acts help to deepen the sense of connection, wonder, and gratitude that Christmas embodies.

The tales of Yuletide spirits remind us that Christmas is not just a time of merriment but also a season of reflection, transformation, and the recognition of the unseen forces that shape our lives. From the joyous to the eerie, these spirits teach us to cherish the light, acknowledge the shadows, and embrace the magic that comes with the turning of the year.

Part 3: *Festive Feasts: Recipes and Tales from the Christmas Table*

Chapter 11: Grandma's Secret Recipe

The scent of cinnamon, cloves, and fresh-baked cookies filling the air, the bubbling of a pot of mulled wine on the stove, the golden crust of a freshly baked pie—these are the sensory delights that make the holiday season feel so warm and inviting. Behind each of these culinary traditions lies a story, a cherished memory, often passed down through generations. In this chapter, we'll explore a collection of holiday recipes, each accompanied by its own backstory. These are the kinds of dishes that have graced countless holiday tables, brought people together, and added a special touch of magic to Christmas celebrations.

1. Grandma Maeve's Mulled Wine
Backstory:

Grandma Maeve grew up in the cold hills of northern Europe, where winter nights could be bitterly cold and dark. Every Christmas Eve, she would prepare a pot of mulled wine to warm the hands and hearts of her family and neighbors. She learned the recipe from her own grandmother, who had used it as a remedy to keep the winter blues at bay. Maeve always added a secret blend of spices that made her mulled wine unforgettable. Her family would gather around the fire, sipping the hot, spiced drink while sharing stories and laughter. Over time, her mulled wine became a symbol of comfort and warmth, and the recipe was passed down through the generations.

Recipe: Grandma Maeve's Mulled Wine
Ingredients:

- 1 bottle of red wine (a medium-bodied variety like Merlot or Shiraz)
- 1/4 cup brandy (optional for extra warmth)
- 1/4 cup honey or sugar (adjust to taste)
- 1 orange, sliced into rounds
- 1 lemon, sliced into rounds
- 2 cinnamon sticks
- 5 cloves
- 3 star anise
- 1/2 teaspoon grated nutmeg
- 1 vanilla bean, split (or 1 teaspoon vanilla extract)
- Fresh cranberries or additional citrus slices for garnish

Instructions:

1. In a large pot, combine the wine, brandy (if using), honey or sugar, and all the spices.
2. Add the orange and lemon slices, stirring gently.
3. Warm the mixture over low heat. Do not let it boil, as this will burn off the alcohol and alter the flavor. Heat for about 20 minutes, stirring occasionally.
4. Taste the wine and add more honey or sugar if desired.
5. Remove the pot from heat and let the wine steep for another 5 minutes.
6. Strain out the spices and fruit slices. Pour the mulled wine into mugs and garnish with fresh cranberries or citrus slices.
7. Serve hot and enjoy the warmth of the holiday season!

Tips: If you prefer a non-alcoholic version, use grape juice instead of wine, and omit the brandy.

2. Nana Rosa's Almond Crescent Cookies
Backstory:

Nana Rosa came from a long line of bakers, and every year, she made dozens of her famous almond crescent cookies for family and friends. These delicate, buttery cookies, with their melt-in-your-mouth texture and dusting of powdered sugar, were a highlight of the holiday season. The recipe, originally from her mother in Italy, was said to bring good fortune to anyone who baked it with love. Nana Rosa would shape each crescent by hand, humming softly to herself, filling the kitchen with the sweet smell of almonds and the promise of a magical Christmas. She believed that sharing these cookies was more than a tradition; it was a way to spread joy and warmth to everyone around her.

Recipe: Nana Rosa's Almond Crescent Cookies
Ingredients:

- 1 cup (2 sticks) unsalted butter, softened
- 1/2 cup powdered sugar (plus extra for dusting)
- 1 teaspoon vanilla extract
- 1/2 teaspoon almond extract
- 1 1/2 cups all-purpose flour
- 1 cup finely ground almonds (or almond flour)
- A pinch of salt

Instructions:

1. Preheat the oven to 350°F (175°C) and line a baking sheet with parchment paper.
2. In a large mixing bowl, beat the softened butter and powdered sugar until light and fluffy.
3. Add the vanilla and almond extracts, mixing until well combined.
4. In a separate bowl, whisk together the flour, ground almonds, and salt.

5. Gradually add the dry ingredients to the butter mixture, stirring until a soft dough forms.

6. Scoop out small portions of dough and shape them into crescent moons. Place them on the prepared baking sheet, spacing them about an inch apart.

7. Bake for 12-15 minutes, or until the edges are lightly golden. Be careful not to overbake, as the cookies should remain tender.

8. Allow the cookies to cool for a few minutes on the baking sheet, then roll them in powdered sugar while still warm. Once they've cooled completely, dust them with additional powdered sugar for a snowy finish.

9. Serve with tea or coffee, and enjoy the tradition of a sweet holiday treat.

Tip: Store these cookies in an airtight container; they'll keep for up to two weeks and even improve in flavor as they rest.

3. Aunt Ethel's Sticky Toffee Pudding
Backstory:

Aunt Ethel was known for her love of sweets and her generosity in the kitchen. Each year, she would bake her famous sticky toffee pudding, a rich, dense cake soaked in a luscious toffee sauce. The recipe was a closely guarded family secret, passed down from her grandmother, who had made it during the Great Depression as a way to bring comfort and cheer during hard times. Aunt Ethel would serve the pudding warm, with a generous dollop of whipped cream or vanilla ice cream, transforming an ordinary winter night into an unforgettable Christmas feast.

Recipe: Aunt Ethel's Sticky Toffee Pudding
Ingredients:
For the pudding:

- 1 cup chopped dates
- 1 cup boiling water
- 1 teaspoon baking soda
- 1/2 cup unsalted butter, softened
- 3/4 cup granulated sugar
- 2 large eggs
- 1 teaspoon vanilla extract
- 1 1/4 cups all-purpose flour
- 1 1/2 teaspoons baking powder
- A pinch of salt

For the toffee sauce:

- 1/2 cup unsalted butter
- 1 cup brown sugar, packed
- 3/4 cup heavy cream

- 1 teaspoon vanilla extract
- A pinch of salt

Instructions:

1. **Prepare the pudding:** Preheat the oven to 350°F (175°C) and butter an 8-inch square baking dish.
2. Place the chopped dates in a small bowl and pour the boiling water over them. Stir in the baking soda and set aside to cool.
3. In a large mixing bowl, beat the butter and sugar until light and creamy. Add the eggs one at a time, beating well after each addition. Stir in the vanilla extract.
4. In a separate bowl, whisk together the flour, baking powder, and salt.
5. Gradually add the flour mixture to the butter mixture, alternating with the date mixture, and stir until just combined.
6. Pour the batter into the prepared baking dish and smooth the top. Bake for 30-35 minutes, or until a toothpick inserted into the center comes out clean.
7. **Make the toffee sauce:** While the pudding is baking, combine the butter, brown sugar, cream, vanilla extract, and salt in a saucepan. Cook over medium heat, stirring constantly until the mixture comes to a gentle boil. Reduce the heat and simmer for 2-3 minutes until the sauce thickens slightly.
8. Remove the pudding from the oven and poke holes across the top using a skewer or fork. Pour half of the toffee sauce over the pudding while it's still warm, allowing it to soak in.
9. Serve the pudding warm, topped with the remaining toffee sauce. For an extra indulgence, add a scoop of vanilla ice cream or a dollop of whipped cream.

Tip: You can make the pudding a day in advance and reheat it in the oven before serving. The flavors will deepen, making it even more delicious!

4. Grandma Elsie's Gingerbread Men
Backstory:

Grandma Elsie had a knack for turning the simplest ingredients into something extraordinary. Her gingerbread men were more than just cookies; they were tiny pieces of art, each one carefully decorated with icing, buttons, and smiles. Every Christmas, the family would gather in her kitchen to bake and decorate these gingerbread men, laughing and telling stories as they worked. The scent of ginger, cinnamon, and cloves would fill the house, marking the official start of the holiday season. Grandma Elsie always said that the secret to her gingerbread was a pinch of love added to each batch. Now, it's a tradition that her grandchildren carry on every year.

Recipe: Grandma Elsie's Gingerbread Men
Ingredients:

- 3 cups all-purpose flour
- 1 teaspoon baking soda
- 1/4 teaspoon baking powder
- 1/2 teaspoon salt
- 1 tablespoon ground ginger
- 2 teaspoons ground cinnamon
- 1/4 teaspoon ground cloves
- 1/2 cup (1 stick) unsalted butter, softened
- 1/2 cup dark brown sugar, packed
- 2/3 cup molasses
- 1 large egg
- 1 teaspoon vanilla extract
- Royal icing, candies, and sprinkles for decorating

Instructions:

1. In a large bowl, whisk together the flour, baking soda, baking powder, salt, ginger, cinnamon, and cloves. Set aside.
2. In a separate mixing bowl, beat the butter and brown sugar until light and fluffy. Add the molasses, egg, and vanilla extract, beating until well combined.
3. Gradually add the dry ingredients to the wet mixture, stirring until a soft dough forms.
4. Divide the dough in half, flatten each half into a disk, wrap in plastic wrap, and refrigerate for at least 2 hours (or overnight) to firm up.
5. Preheat the oven to 350°F (175°C) and line baking sheets with parchment paper.
6. On a lightly floured surface, roll out the dough to about 1/4-inch thickness. Use gingerbread man cookie cutters to cut out shapes, placing them on the prepared baking sheets.
7. Bake for 8-10 minutes, or until the edges are firm. Let the cookies cool on the baking sheets for a few minutes before transferring them to wire racks to cool completely.
8. Decorate the gingerbread men with royal icing, candies, and sprinkles to give them their unique personalities. Let the icing set before serving.

Tip: Store decorated gingerbread men in an airtight container for up to a week. They also make wonderful gifts when wrapped in festive bags or boxes!

The Joy of Sharing Family Recipes

The recipes in this chapter represent more than just food; they are pieces of history, love, and tradition passed down through the generations. Each dish carries the warmth of family gatherings, the joy of creation, and the magic of the holiday season. As you prepare these recipes, take a moment to reflect on the stories behind them and the memories you'll create as you share them with loved ones.

Whether it's the rich aroma of mulled wine wafting through the kitchen, the sweet taste of almond crescent cookies, the comforting indulgence of sticky toffee pudding, or the fun of decorating gingerbread men, these recipes are an invitation to celebrate the heart of Christmas: togetherness, love, and the simple joys of home. May you find comfort and delight in these cherished family secrets, and may they add a special touch of magic to your holiday season.

Chapter 12: The Gingerbread Chronicles

Gingerbread houses, with their intricately decorated roofs, candy-laden walls, and sugar-glazed windows, are one of the most enchanting symbols of the holiday season. They stand as edible works of art, lovingly crafted by both amateur and master bakers alike, often becoming the centerpiece of festive gatherings. However, the tradition of gingerbread goes far beyond its use as a simple treat. It holds a rich history filled with lore, artistry, and cultural significance. In this chapter, we'll explore the origins of gingerbread and the tradition of creating gingerbread houses, before delving into a magical story set in a gingerbread village.

The History of Gingerbread

Gingerbread has a long and storied history that dates back to ancient times. The earliest known use of ginger in baking can be traced to ancient Greece and Egypt, where it was used to create spiced cakes for religious ceremonies. However, it was during the Middle Ages that gingerbread, as we know it, began to take shape in Europe. Crusaders returning from the Middle East brought ginger and other spices with them, and these ingredients quickly found their way into the kitchens of European bakers.

Initially, gingerbread was not the soft, chewy cookie we associate with the holidays. It was made using honey and spices, often pressed into elaborate molds to create intricate designs, and baked into a hard, crisp texture. Gingerbread was prized not only for its flavor but also for its preservative properties. The combination of honey, sugar, and spices allowed it to last longer than other baked goods, making it ideal for long journeys or for keeping through the winter months.

By the 16th century, gingerbread had become a beloved treat across Europe. In England, it was referred to as "gingerbread" and was sold at fairs in various shapes, including animals, flowers, and even human figures known as "gingerbread men." Queen Elizabeth I is credited with popularizing the gingerbread man, as she had cookies decorated to resemble visiting dignitaries at her court.

The Birth of the Gingerbread House

The tradition of making gingerbread houses is believed to have originated in Germany during the early 1800s. It was inspired by the Brothers Grimm's fairy tale, *Hansel and Gretel*, in which two children find a house made entirely of sweets in the woods. The story captured the imagination of bakers, who began creating elaborately decorated houses from gingerbread, icing, and candies. These houses, known as *Lebkuchenhäuser*, became popular during the Christmas season, symbolizing warmth, comfort, and the joy of festive indulgence.

German immigrants brought the tradition of gingerbread houses to America, where it flourished and evolved. Today, gingerbread houses range from simple cottages to grand, architectural marvels, often adorned with gumdrops, candy canes, chocolate, and powdered sugar snow. Building a gingerbread house has become a beloved family activity, a way to celebrate creativity and togetherness during the holidays.

Crafting Your Gingerbread House

Building a gingerbread house requires patience, a touch of imagination, and, most importantly, a sense of fun. Here's how to create a classic gingerbread house:

Ingredients for the Gingerbread:

- 1 cup (2 sticks) unsalted butter, softened
- 1 cup granulated sugar
- 1 cup molasses
- 2 large eggs
- 5 cups all-purpose flour
- 1 teaspoon baking soda
- 1 tablespoon ground ginger
- 1 tablespoon ground cinnamon
- 1 teaspoon ground cloves
- 1/2 teaspoon salt

Royal Icing (for assembling and decorating):

- 3 large egg whites
- 1/2 teaspoon cream of tartar
- 4 cups powdered sugar

Assorted Candies for Decorating:

- Gumdrops, candy canes, peppermints, licorice, chocolate pieces, and more!

Instructions:

1. **Prepare the Gingerbread Dough:**
   - In a large mixing bowl, beat the softened butter and sugar until light and fluffy. Add the molasses and eggs, mixing well.
   - In a separate bowl, whisk together the flour, baking soda, ginger, cinnamon, cloves, and salt.
   - Gradually add the dry ingredients to the butter mixture, stirring until a stiff dough forms. Divide the dough into two disks, wrap in plastic wrap, and chill in the refrigerator for at least 1 hour.

2. **Roll and Cut the Gingerbread:**
   - Preheat the oven to 350°F (175°C) and line baking sheets with parchment paper.
   - Roll out the chilled dough on a floured surface to about 1/4-inch thickness. Use a sharp knife or a gingerbread house template to cut out the pieces for your house (walls, roof, door, windows).
   - Place the cut-out pieces on the baking sheets and bake for 12-15 minutes, or until firm. Let them cool completely on a wire rack before assembling.

3. **Make the Royal Icing:**
   - In a mixing bowl, beat the egg whites and cream of tartar until frothy. Gradually add the powdered sugar, beating until the icing is thick and smooth.
   - Transfer the icing to a piping bag for easy assembly and decorating.

4. Assemble the House:

- Use the royal icing to glue the walls of the house together, holding each piece in place for a minute or two until it sets. Attach the roof pieces last. Allow the house to dry for at least 1 hour before decorating

-
-
- **5. Decorate:**
  - Let your imagination run wild! Use the royal icing to attach candies, chocolate, sprinkles, and any other decorations to your gingerbread house. Add gumdrops for bushes, candy canes for pillars, and licorice ropes for trim.

Tip: For an extra magical touch, dust the completed house with powdered sugar to create a snow-covered effect.

A Story Set in a Gingerbread Village: The Enchanted Gingerbread Village

In a land not found on any map, nestled amidst rolling hills of powdered sugar and forests of candy canes, lies the Enchanted Gingerbread Village. Each house in this village is made entirely of gingerbread, with roofs of peppermint tiles, windows of spun sugar, and chimneys puffing the sweet aroma of cinnamon and cloves. Gumdrop bushes line the cobblestone streets, and frosting icicles dangle from the eaves of every home. During the winter, snow made of powdered sugar blankets the village, giving it a magical, twinkling appearance under the light of candy stars.

The village was home to a small, merry community of gingerbread people. They were a joyous lot, known for their love of music, baking, and storytelling. But above all, they cherished the annual *Festival of Frosting*, a time when the villagers would gather to build new houses and celebrate the magic that made their village come alive.

However, one year, as the Festival of Frosting approached, the village faced an unexpected challenge. A strange, bitter wind had begun to blow through the land, drying out the frosting and turning the gingerbread houses brittle. The villagers were worried; without the protection of their sweet, sturdy homes, they feared they might crumble to dust.

In the center of the village stood a grand gingerbread house known as the *Sugarplum Hall*, home to the village elder, Granny Nutmeg. Granny Nutmeg was wise in the ways of baking magic and had lived through many winters. She gathered the villagers around and said, "There is only one way to save our village. We must find the *Golden Spice*, a magical ingredient that can restore the sweetness and strength to our gingerbread."

"But where do we find the Golden Spice?" asked Pip, a young gingerbread boy with a peppermint hat.

Granny Nutmeg pointed to the distant hills. "The Golden Spice grows in the heart of the *Spicewood Forest*, beyond the Valley of Sugar Crystals. It will be a long and difficult journey, but we must bring it back before the festival begins."

Pip volunteered to embark on the quest, and with the villagers' blessings, he set off. As he ventured through the Valley of Sugar Crystals, the wind howled around him, threatening to break off pieces of his gingerbread limbs. But Pip pressed on, thinking of the village and the warmth of their homes.

After days of travel, he reached the edge of the Spicewood Forest, a place where the air was filled with the scent of cinnamon, nutmeg, and cloves. Deep within the forest, he found the source of the magic—the *Golden Spice Tree*, its branches heavy with sparkling, golden ginger roots.

With careful hands, Pip gathered the ginger roots, wrapping them in a cloth to keep their magic safe. As he turned to leave, he heard a voice whisper through the trees, "Only those with sweetness in their hearts can carry the Golden Spice."

Pip looked around but saw no one. He then realized it was the spirit of the forest speaking to him. He nodded solemnly. "I carry this spice for my village, to bring warmth and joy back to our homes," he said. With that, the forest seemed to glow brighter, and the winds calmed.

Pip returned to the village just as the Festival of Frosting was about to begin. The villagers cheered as he approached, holding up the cloth with the Golden Spice inside. Granny Nutmeg took the spice and mixed it into the dough for the new houses. As they baked, a warm, golden light filled the village, and the air grew sweet with the scent of ginger and cloves.

The new houses were strong, their walls gleaming with a rich, honeyed color. The villagers worked together, decorating them with frosting and candies, singing songs of joy and gratitude. That night, as the

Festival of Frosting commenced, the village glowed under the candy stars, safe and warm once more.

From that day on, the Enchanted Gingerbread Village flourished. And every year, as they celebrated the Festival of Frosting, they remembered Pip's bravery and the magic of the Golden Spice that kept their homes sweet and strong. It became a tale passed down through generations, reminding everyone that the strength of the village came not just from the gingerbread but from the love and care they shared with one another.

The Sweet Tradition of Gingerbread

The tradition of making gingerbread houses is more than a culinary art; it is an expression of creativity, love, and togetherness. Whether simple cottages or elaborate mansions, each gingerbread house tells a story, becoming a part of the memories that warm our hearts during the coldest season of the year.

As you craft your gingerbread house, remember the story of the Enchanted Gingerbread Village and the magic that happens when we create something with care and share it with those we love. In every sprinkle of sugar and every piece of candy, there lies the essence of the holidays—sweet, enduring, and filled with joy.

Chapter 13: Feasts of Yore

Christmas feasts have long been a central part of holiday celebrations, serving as the gathering point for family, friends, and neighbors to share in the bounty of the season. From grand medieval banquets in stone castles to humble, hearty meals in the countryside, these feasts brought warmth and joy to the darkest days of winter. The history of Christmas feasting is rich with tradition, each dish steeped in culture, folklore, and the spirit of giving. In this chapter, we will delve into the ancient Christmas feasts of yore, exploring the customs, recipes, and stories that have made their way to modern holiday tables. We'll journey from England's grand banquets to the simple but meaningful meals of Scandinavia and Eastern Europe.

The Origins of Christmas Feasting

The tradition of Christmas feasting can be traced back to ancient winter solstice celebrations. Before Christianity spread through Europe, many pagan cultures held midwinter feasts to honor the return of the sun after the longest night of the year. These feasts celebrated the abundance of the harvest, and people gathered to eat, drink, and be merry as a way to ward off the cold and darkness.

With the Christianization of Europe, many of these customs were incorporated into the Christmas holiday. The day of feasting moved to December 25th, in honor of the birth of Christ, and the festive meal became a way to celebrate both the spiritual and earthly blessings of the season. Medieval Christmas feasts were particularly grand, often lasting for several days and featuring a lavish array of meats, pies, breads, and sweets. Over the centuries, these traditions evolved, influenced by regional customs, ingredients, and the ever-changing tides of history.

A Medieval English Christmas Feast

During the Middle Ages, Christmas was marked by magnificent feasts, particularly in the grand halls of castles and manors across England. The feast often began on Christmas Eve and continued for the Twelve Days of Christmas, culminating on Twelfth Night (January 6th). The centerpiece of the feast was usually a roasted animal—sometimes an entire boar, peacock, or goose—surrounded by an array of sides, sauces, and sweets.

The Tale of the Boar's Head:

One of the most famous dishes at medieval Christmas feasts was the boar's head. This dish was steeped in both practical and symbolic importance. In pagan tradition, the boar was a symbol of strength and fertility, and the serving of its head at a feast was meant to honor the gods and ensure prosperity in the coming year. As the custom became part of Christmas celebrations, the boar's head also came to symbolize the triumph of good over evil, aligning with the Christian theme of the holiday.

In grand feasts, the boar's head was often presented with great ceremony, garnished with fruits, herbs, and gilded accents. It would be paraded into the dining hall on a silver platter, accompanied by musicians and a song of praise known as the "Boar's Head Carol." Although the tradition of serving an actual boar's head has faded over the centuries, the carol is still sung in some parts of England as a nod to this ancient custom.

Recipe: Honey-Roasted Pork with Apples (Inspired by the Boar's Head)

While a whole boar's head may be impractical today, this honey-roasted pork dish captures the essence of the medieval feast with its blend of savory and sweet flavors.

Ingredients:

- 1 pork loin roast (about 3-4 lbs)
- Salt and pepper, to taste
- 2 tablespoons olive oil
- 1/4 cup honey
- 1/4 cup apple cider vinegar
- 2 large apples, cored and sliced
- 1 onion, sliced
- 2 cloves garlic, minced
- 1 tablespoon fresh rosemary, chopped (or 1 teaspoon dried)
- 1/2 teaspoon ground cloves
- 1/4 teaspoon nutmeg

Instructions:

1. Preheat the oven to 375°F (190°C).
2. Season the pork loin with salt and pepper. In a large oven-safe skillet or roasting pan, heat the olive oil over medium-high heat. Sear the pork on all sides until browned.
3. In a small bowl, whisk together the honey and apple cider vinegar. Pour the mixture over the pork.
4. Add the apple slices, onion, garlic, rosemary, cloves, and nutmeg to the pan, arranging them around the pork.
5. Transfer the pan to the oven and roast for about 1 hour, basting occasionally with the pan juices. The pork is done when it reaches an internal temperature of 145°F (63°C).

6. Remove the pork from the oven and let it rest for 10 minutes before slicing. Serve with the apples and onions, drizzled with the pan juices.

The Yule Feast of Scandinavia

In Scandinavian countries, the *Yule* feast, known as *Jól* in Old Norse, was a central part of the winter solstice celebrations. Yule was originally a pagan festival celebrating the rebirth of the sun, marked by feasting, toasts, and offerings to the gods. When Christianity spread through the region, Yule became intertwined with Christmas, but many of its ancient customs were retained, including the hearty, communal feast.

The Legend of the Yule Goat:

An iconic figure in Scandinavian Christmas lore is the Yule Goat (*Julbocken*), a symbol of fertility and protection. In ancient times, a person dressed as a goat would go from house to house, demanding food and drink—a practice that evolved into the modern tradition of caroling. The Yule Goat was also said to deliver gifts, a role that later shifted to Santa Claus. Today, straw goats are still used as Christmas decorations, keeping the spirit of this age-old custom alive.

One of the traditional dishes served during the Yule feast is *Julskinka* (Christmas ham), accompanied by rich sides like potato gratin, pickled herring, and rye bread. To finish the meal, families enjoy *Risgrynsgröt* (rice pudding), often hiding an almond inside. It is said that whoever finds the almond in their serving will have good luck in the coming year.

Recipe: Scandinavian Rice Pudding (Risgrynsgröt)
This creamy, fragrant rice pudding is a comforting treat, perfect for sharing on a cold winter's night. Its simplicity belies the rich history and warmth it brings to the table.
Ingredients:

- 1 cup short-grain rice (such as Arborio)
- 2 cups water
- 4 cups whole milk
- 1/4 teaspoon salt
- 1 cinnamon stick
- 1/4 cup sugar
- 1 teaspoon vanilla extract
- 1 whole almond (optional)
- Ground cinnamon and sugar, for serving

Instructions:

1. In a large saucepan, combine the rice and water. Bring to a boil over medium heat, then reduce the heat to low and simmer for about 10 minutes, or until the water is absorbed.
2. Add the milk, salt, and cinnamon stick to the rice. Cook over low heat, stirring occasionally, for 30-40 minutes, or until the rice is tender and the mixture is creamy.
3. Stir in the sugar and vanilla extract. If using, drop the whole almond into the pudding and stir gently to hide it.
4. Serve the pudding warm, sprinkled with cinnamon and sugar. For an extra touch of holiday tradition, have each guest search their serving for the hidden almond!

Eastern European Christmas Feasts: The Twelve Dishes of Koliada

In Eastern Europe, particularly in countries like Poland, Ukraine, and Lithuania, Christmas Eve is marked by a special feast known as the *Holy Supper* or *Koliada*. This meal consists of twelve dishes, symbolizing the twelve apostles, and is traditionally meatless to honor the fast before Christmas. The table is often set with a white cloth and hay underneath, representing the manger in which Jesus was born.

The Story of the Kutya:

One of the most important dishes in the Koliada feast is *kutya*, a sweet, grain-based pudding made with wheat berries, honey, and poppy seeds. According to tradition, the head of the household would toss a spoonful of kutya at the ceiling. If the kutya stuck, it was believed that the family would have a bountiful harvest in the coming year. Kutya embodies the themes of unity, hope, and the continuity of life through its simple, nourishing ingredients.

Recipe: Traditional Kutya
Ingredients:

- 1 cup wheat berries (or barley)
- 4 cups water
- 1/2 cup honey
- 1/2 cup poppy seeds
- 1/2 cup chopped nuts (walnuts, almonds, or hazelnuts)
- 1/4 cup raisins or dried fruit
- A pinch of salt

Instructions:

1. Rinse the wheat berries under cold water. Place them in a large saucepan with the water and a pinch of salt. Bring to a boil, then reduce the heat and simmer for about 1 hour, or until the grains are tender. Drain any excess water.
2. While the wheat is cooking, soak the poppy seeds in hot water for about 30 minutes. Drain, then grind the seeds using a food processor or mortar and pestle.
3. In a large mixing bowl, combine the cooked wheat, honey, poppy seeds, nuts, and dried fruit. Mix well until all ingredients are evenly distributed.
4. Serve the kutya in small bowls, either warm or at room temperature, as a symbolic dish of the Koliada feast.

The Joy of Feasting: A Timeless Tradition

From the grand halls of medieval England to the cozy homes of Eastern Europe, Christmas feasts have always been about more than just the food. They are moments of togetherness, where stories are shared, traditions are upheld, and the bonds of family and friendship are strengthened. Each dish, whether it's a honey-roasted pork, a bowl of creamy rice pudding, or a humble serving of kutya, carries the essence of the season—warmth, gratitude, and the hope for a prosperous future.

As you prepare and enjoy your own Christmas feast, may you be reminded of the ancient customs and stories that have shaped our celebrations today. In every bite, savor not just the flavors, but the history, the love, and the joy that have made these feasts of yore so timeless.

Chapter 14: Candied Delights

There's something magical about Christmas sweets. The shimmer of sugar crystals, the crunch of caramelized nuts, the soft chew of taffy—all bring to life the flavors and joy of the season. Behind these sweet treats lies a tradition of candy-making that dates back centuries, passed down through generations to warm hearts and celebrate the spirit of giving. In this chapter, we'll explore the world of traditional Christmas sweets, providing you with recipes and the know-how to create your own candied delights at home. Intertwined with this guide is the charming tale of a candy maker whose dream brought a little extra magic to his village during the holiday season.

A Candy Maker's Dream

In a small, snow-covered village nestled among pine forests and winding rivers, there lived a candy maker named Fritz. His shop, "Fritz's Sweet Emporium," stood at the heart of the village square, its windows adorned with colorful candies and confections that glistened in the winter sun. Fritz was not just any candy maker; he was known throughout the land for his talent in crafting the most exquisite sweets. His hands could twist caramel into delicate flowers, mold chocolate into whimsical shapes, and coat nuts with a perfect, crisp shell of sugar.

But as Christmas approached one year, Fritz found himself in a quandary. The village had been through a difficult time; the winter had been harsh, and many villagers were struggling. Fritz wanted to bring them joy, to remind them of the warmth and magic of Christmas through his candies. Yet, he didn't know how to create something truly special that could lift everyone's spirits.

One snowy evening, as Fritz sat by the fire in his cozy shop, a vision came to him in a dream. He saw a wondrous land made entirely of sweets: peppermint forests, chocolate rivers, and gingerbread cottages covered in sugared fruit. In the center of this land stood a grand candy tree, its branches heavy with glistening candies of every kind. The tree glowed with a golden light, casting warmth and joy over the entire landscape.

When Fritz awoke, he was filled with inspiration. "I will make my own Candied Delights for the village," he thought, "a collection of sweets so wonderful that it will bring joy and warmth to every home." With that, he set to work, using his dream as a guide to create the most magical candies he had ever made.

Traditional Christmas Sweets and Their Crafting

The art of candy-making is an age-old tradition, requiring patience, skill, and a bit of magic. Below, you will find recipes for some of the most beloved Christmas sweets, from sugar-dusted fruits to peppermint swirls. Each recipe captures the essence of the season, allowing you to create your own collection of candied delights.

1. **Candied Orange Peel**

In many cultures, citrus fruits symbolize the brightness and warmth of the sun, especially during the dark days of winter. Candied orange peel is a traditional Christmas treat that embodies this symbolism, combining the tartness of citrus with the sweetness of sugar for a chewy, flavorful delight.

Ingredients:

- 4 large oranges
- 2 cups granulated sugar (plus extra for coating)
- 1 cup water

Instructions:

1. Cut the oranges into quarters and remove the flesh, leaving the peel intact. Slice the peel into thin strips.
2. Place the orange peels in a medium saucepan and cover them with water. Bring to a boil, then reduce the heat and simmer for 5 minutes. Drain and repeat this process two more times to remove the bitterness.
3. In a clean saucepan, combine 2 cups of sugar and 1 cup of water. Stir over medium heat until the sugar dissolves. Add the orange peel and bring to a simmer.
4. Cook the peels for about 45 minutes, stirring occasionally, until they become translucent.
5. Using a slotted spoon, transfer the peels to a wire rack to cool slightly. While still warm, roll them in granulated sugar to coat.
6. Allow the candied peels to dry for several hours. Store in an airtight container for up to two weeks.

Tip: Dip one end of each candied peel in melted dark chocolate for an extra indulgent treat!

2. Caramelized Nuts

Caramelized nuts, whether they be almonds, hazelnuts, or pecans, are a classic Christmas market treat. Their crunchy texture and sweet, toasty flavor evoke the festive atmosphere of the season.

Ingredients:

- 2 cups whole nuts (almonds, pecans, hazelnuts)
- 1 cup granulated sugar
- 1/4 cup water
- 1/2 teaspoon cinnamon
- A pinch of salt

Instructions:

1. Line a baking sheet with parchment paper and set aside.
2. In a large, heavy-bottomed saucepan, combine the sugar, water, cinnamon, and salt. Stir over medium heat until the sugar dissolves and the mixture comes to a simmer.
3. Add the nuts and continue cooking, stirring constantly. The sugar will begin to crystallize and coat the nuts.
4. Keep stirring until the sugar melts and caramelizes, turning a golden brown and giving the nuts a glossy finish.
5. Quickly spread the nuts onto the prepared baking sheet. Use a spatula to separate them while they are still warm to prevent clumping.
6. Allow the nuts to cool completely before storing them in an airtight container.

Tip: For a twist, add a dash of cayenne pepper to the sugar mixture for a hint of spice.

3. Peppermint Swirl Candies

The peppermint swirl candy is as iconic to Christmas as the scent of pine. These sweets are surprisingly simple to make and bring a nostalgic, homemade charm to the candy bowl.

Ingredients:

- 2 cups granulated sugar
- 1/2 cup light corn syrup
- 1/4 cup water
- 1/2 teaspoon peppermint extract
- Red food coloring

Instructions:

1. In a medium saucepan, combine the sugar, corn syrup, and water. Stir over medium heat until the sugar dissolves.
2. Increase the heat to medium-high and cook without stirring until the mixture reaches 300°F (150°C) on a candy thermometer (the hard crack stage).
3. Remove the saucepan from the heat and quickly stir in the peppermint extract. Pour half of the mixture onto a baking sheet lined with parchment paper.
4. Add a few drops of red food coloring to the remaining mixture in the saucepan. Pour this mixture onto the other side of the baking sheet.
5. Once the candy is cool enough to handle but still pliable, pull and stretch both colors separately until they become glossy. Twist the red and clear candy ropes together to form a swirl, then cut into small pieces with oiled scissors.
6. Allow the candies to cool completely. Wrap each piece in parchment paper or cellophane for easy gifting.

Tip: Work quickly with the candy once it's cool enough to handle, as it hardens fast!

4. Marzipan Fruit

Marzipan, a confection made from almond paste and sugar, has been a part of Christmas traditions for centuries. Shaping marzipan into miniature fruits and vegetables is a delightful activity for both adults and children, bringing a touch of artistry to the holiday table.

Ingredients:

- 1 cup almond flour
- 1 cup powdered sugar
- 1-2 tablespoons water
- Food coloring (red, yellow, green)
- Cloves, cinnamon sticks, or dried herbs (for decoration)

Instructions:

1. In a mixing bowl, combine the almond flour and powdered sugar. Add water, a few drops at a time, and knead the mixture until it forms a smooth, pliable dough.
2. Divide the marzipan into small portions and tint each with different colors using food coloring. Knead until the colors are evenly distributed.
3. Shape the marzipan into miniature fruits such as apples, oranges, bananas, and pears. Use cloves, cinnamon sticks, or dried herbs to create stems and leaves.
4. Arrange the marzipan fruits on a serving plate or use them to decorate cakes and desserts.

Tip: Dust the marzipan fruits with a little cocoa powder or ground cinnamon to add a realistic texture.

The Candy Maker's Surprise

As Fritz worked late into the night, his shop filled with the aroma of sugar, citrus, and peppermint. He crafted candied orange peels, caramelized nuts, peppermint swirls, and marzipan fruits, each confection a reflection of the dream that had inspired him. He carefully wrapped the sweets in parchment paper and tied them with ribbons, creating little packages of joy.

The next morning, Fritz stepped out into the snowy village, his arms laden with baskets of candies. He went from house to house, leaving a bundle of sweets on each doorstep. When the villagers awoke, they found Fritz's Candied Delights waiting for them, their spirits instantly lifted by the thoughtful surprise.

Word of Fritz's magical candies spread, and soon the entire village was abuzz with laughter and cheer. The candies were shared among families, given as gifts to friends, and enjoyed at every holiday gathering. That Christmas, the village felt warmer, brighter, and filled with the spirit of giving that Fritz had poured into his sweets.

From that year on, the villagers eagerly awaited Fritz's Candied Delights, and the tradition grew. The children of the village began visiting Fritz's shop each Christmas Eve to help him make the candies, learning the art of candy-making and the joy of sharing something sweet with others. In time, "Fritz's Sweet Emporium" became known not just for its confections, but for the love and magic that went into each piece.

Candied Delights: A Celebration of Sweetness

The joy of Christmas candy-making lies not only in the delicious results but also in the care and creativity that go into each confection. Whether you're coating orange peels in sugar, caramelizing nuts, twisting peppermint into swirls, or shaping marzipan fruits, you're partaking in an age-old tradition of spreading sweetness and delight.

As you craft these candies, think of the candy maker's dream and the happiness that a simple treat can bring. Share your creations with family, friends, or neighbors, and let the warmth of your candied delights fill hearts and homes with the magic of Christmas.

Chapter 15: The Mistletoe Kitchen

In the warmth of the kitchen, where the crackle of the hearth meets the sweet aroma of spices and herbs, lies the heart of many Christmas traditions. This chapter explores the mystical side of holiday cooking, drawing on folklore and ancient beliefs that have long surrounded some of our favorite ingredients. From recipes that invoke love and friendship to dishes that symbolize protection and good fortune, the *Mistletoe Kitchen* brings together a collection of magical recipes steeped in yuletide lore. Inspired by the mistletoe—a plant long associated with love, healing, and enchantment—these recipes are crafted with intention, aiming to bring people together in joy and harmony.

The Mystical Power of Holiday Ingredients

Before diving into the recipes, it's important to understand that many of the ingredients we use in holiday cooking have their roots in folklore and magical traditions. Long ago, people believed that the foods they consumed could influence their lives, particularly during significant times of the year, like Christmas. Here are a few ingredients and their mystical properties:

- **Mistletoe:** Although not edible, mistletoe has long been associated with love, fertility, and protection. In ancient times, it was hung over doorways to ward off evil spirits and invite good fortune. During the holiday season, it has become a symbol of love and friendship, as couples kiss beneath it for good luck.
- **Cinnamon:** This warm spice is thought to attract prosperity, love, and protection. It's commonly used in Christmas baking to infuse warmth and joy into the home.
- **Nutmeg:** Nutmeg is believed to bring luck, fortune, and harmony. Sprinkling a little nutmeg into food or drink during the holidays is said to attract positivity and protect against misfortune.

- **Rosemary:** Associated with remembrance and friendship, rosemary is often used in holiday meals to honor loved ones and strengthen bonds of friendship.
- **Honey:** Honey symbolizes sweetness and the richness of life. In many cultures, it is seen as a gift of nature that brings love, healing, and prosperity.

With these magical properties in mind, the following recipes are designed to not only nourish the body but also to celebrate the mystical elements of love, friendship, and the season's joy.

1. **Mistletoe Bread (Rosemary & Honey Bread)**

This aromatic bread, infused with rosemary and honey, is inspired by the tradition of hanging mistletoe for love and protection. Baking and sharing this bread symbolizes unity and the strengthening of bonds among friends and family.

Ingredients:

- 3 cups all-purpose flour
- 1 tablespoon sugar
- 1 teaspoon salt
- 1 packet (2 1/4 teaspoons) active dry yeast
- 1 cup warm water (about 110°F/45°C)
- 2 tablespoons honey
- 2 tablespoons olive oil
- 1 tablespoon fresh rosemary, chopped (or 1 teaspoon dried rosemary)
- Extra rosemary sprigs and honey for garnish

Instructions:

1. In a large mixing bowl, combine the flour, sugar, and salt. In a separate small bowl, mix the warm water, yeast, and honey. Let it sit for about 5 minutes until it becomes frothy.
2. Pour the yeast mixture into the dry ingredients. Add the olive oil and chopped rosemary, then mix until a soft dough forms.
3. Turn the dough out onto a floured surface and knead for about 8 minutes until it becomes smooth and elastic.

4. Place the dough in a greased bowl, cover with a clean cloth, and let it rise in a warm place for about 1 hour, or until it doubles in size.

5. Preheat the oven to 375°F (190°C). Punch down the dough and shape it into a round loaf. Place it on a baking sheet lined with parchment paper.

6. Lightly score the top of the loaf with a knife, then brush it with olive oil and sprinkle with extra rosemary. Bake for 25-30 minutes, or until the bread sounds hollow when tapped on the bottom.

7. While the bread is still warm, drizzle a little honey over the top. Serve with butter or a dish of honey for dipping.

Mystical Element: The rosemary in this bread symbolizes love and friendship, while the honey adds sweetness to life's moments. Baking this bread is an act of intention, creating warmth and unity for those who share it.

2. Spiced Friendship Cider

Cider has been enjoyed during the winter months for centuries, often flavored with spices known to attract warmth and positivity. This mulled cider recipe brings together friends and family in the spirit of love and togetherness.

Ingredients:

- 1 gallon apple cider (or apple juice)
- 2 cinnamon sticks
- 1 teaspoon whole cloves
- 1 teaspoon allspice berries
- 1 orange, sliced
- 1 apple, sliced
- 1/4 cup honey
- A pinch of nutmeg

Instructions:

1. In a large pot, combine the apple cider, cinnamon sticks, cloves, allspice berries, orange slices, apple slices, honey, and nutmeg.
2. Bring the mixture to a simmer over medium heat. Reduce the heat to low and let the cider gently simmer for 30 minutes, allowing the flavors to meld.
3. Strain the cider to remove the spices and fruit slices. Serve warm in mugs, garnished with a cinnamon stick or a slice of orange.

Mystical Element: The combination of spices—cinnamon for love and prosperity, cloves for protection, and nutmeg for luck—infuses this cider with warmth and positive energy, making it a perfect drink to share with loved ones during the holiday season.

3. Cinnamon Love Stars (Cinnamon Shortbread Cookies)

These delicate cookies are shaped like stars, a symbol of guidance and light, and spiced with cinnamon to evoke warmth and love. Sharing these cookies with friends or offering them as gifts spreads sweetness and joy.

Ingredients:

- 1 cup (2 sticks) unsalted butter, softened
- 1/2 cup powdered sugar
- 1 teaspoon vanilla extract
- 2 cups all-purpose flour
- 1/2 teaspoon ground cinnamon
- A pinch of salt
- Extra powdered sugar and cinnamon for dusting

Instructions:

1. In a large mixing bowl, beat the softened butter and powdered sugar until light and fluffy. Add the vanilla extract and mix well.
2. In a separate bowl, whisk together the flour, cinnamon, and salt. Gradually add the dry ingredients to the butter mixture, stirring until a soft dough forms.
3. Divide the dough into two disks, wrap in plastic wrap, and chill in the refrigerator for at least 30 minutes.
4. Preheat the oven to 350°F (175°C) and line a baking sheet with parchment paper.
5. Roll out the chilled dough on a lightly floured surface to about 1/4-inch thickness. Use a star-shaped cookie cutter to cut out cookies and place them on the prepared baking sheet.
6. Bake for 10-12 minutes, or until the edges are lightly golden. Allow the cookies to cool on the baking sheet for a few minutes, then transfer them to a wire rack to cool completely.

7. Dust the cooled cookies with a mixture of powdered sugar and cinnamon for a sweet, sparkling finish.

Mystical Element: Shaped like stars, these cookies are a reminder of the guiding light of love and friendship during the holidays. The cinnamon within the cookies is known to attract warmth and affection, making them perfect for sharing.

4. Friendship Wreath Salad (Winter Citrus & Pomegranate Salad)

This vibrant salad, arranged in the shape of a wreath, is not only a feast for the eyes but also a dish that brings health and renewal to the table. The combination of citrus fruits and pomegranate seeds symbolizes abundance, friendship, and the sweetness of life.

Ingredients:

- 2 large oranges, peeled and sliced into rounds
- 2 large grapefruits, peeled and sliced into rounds
- 1 pomegranate, seeds removed
- 1/4 cup fresh mint leaves
- 1 tablespoon honey
- 2 tablespoons olive oil
- 1 tablespoon lemon juice
- Salt and pepper, to taste
- Fresh rosemary sprigs for garnish

Instructions:

1. Arrange the orange and grapefruit slices in a circular pattern on a large serving platter to resemble a wreath.
2. Sprinkle the pomegranate seeds and mint leaves over the citrus slices.
3. In a small bowl, whisk together the honey, olive oil, and lemon juice. Drizzle the dressing over the fruit.
4. Season the salad with a pinch of salt and pepper. Garnish with fresh rosemary sprigs to complete the wreath look.
5. Serve immediately as a refreshing and colorful addition to the holiday feast.

Mystical Element: This wreath salad is a celebration of friendship and abundance. The pomegranate is often associated with fertility and prosperity, while citrus fruits bring brightness and energy. The arrangement in the shape of a wreath symbolizes unity and the circle of life.

5. Mistletoe Hot Chocolate (Rosemary-Infused Hot Chocolate)

Hot chocolate is the epitome of comfort during the holiday season. This unique twist on the classic beverage incorporates rosemary, a herb of remembrance and friendship, to add an unexpected depth of flavor and a touch of magic.

Ingredients:

- 2 cups whole milk
- 1 cup heavy cream
- 8 oz dark chocolate, chopped
- 1 tablespoon sugar
- 1 small sprig of fresh rosemary
- Whipped cream, for topping
- Fresh rosemary and chocolate shavings for garnish

Instructions:

1. In a medium saucepan, combine the milk, heavy cream, and rosemary sprig. Heat over medium heat until it begins to simmer, then remove from heat and let steep for 5 minutes.
2. Remove the rosemary sprig and return the saucepan to medium heat. Add the chopped chocolate and sugar, whisking until the chocolate is melted and the mixture is smooth.
3. Pour the hot chocolate into mugs and top with whipped cream. Garnish with a small sprig of rosemary and chocolate shavings.
4. Serve warm and enjoy the aromatic, herbal twist on this classic drink.

Mystical Element: The infusion of rosemary brings the magic of friendship and remembrance into this comforting drink. Sipping on this hot chocolate with friends or loved ones fosters warmth and connection, embodying the spirit of the season.

Cooking with Heart in The Mistletoe Kitchen

The recipes in the Mistletoe Kitchen are more than just food—they are expressions of love, friendship, and the mystical elements of the holiday season. Each dish carries a story, an intention to nurture the bonds that bring people together. Whether you're baking the aromatic rosemary bread, stirring a pot of spiced cider, or decorating cookies shaped like stars, you're engaging in the ancient tradition of using food to invoke joy, warmth, and harmony.

As you create and share these dishes, remember the magic of the ingredients you're using and the love that goes into each recipe. Let the Mistletoe Kitchen be a place of celebration, where the flavors of the season enhance the moments of togetherness and make every meal a feast for the heart.

Part 4: *Winter Wonderland: Mystical Places and Creatures of Christmas*

Chapter 16: The Enchanted Forest

Deep within the heart of Christmas folklore lies a place of wonder and magic—a mystical forest where the spirit of the season is alive in every tree, creature, and whispering breeze. Known simply as *The Enchanted Forest*, it is a place where legends come to life, where every snowflake glows with a soft light, and where creatures of Christmas lore roam freely. From Santa's reindeer grazing under starlit skies to mischievous elves preparing festive surprises, the forest is a realm of enchantment. This chapter invites you on a journey into the mythical forest, exploring the creatures that dwell there and the stories they have to tell, revealing how their timeless magic has become a part of our Christmas traditions.

The Entrance to the Enchanted Forest

It is said that the entrance to the Enchanted Forest can only be found during the days leading up to Christmas. The forest is hidden from the world of ordinary mortals, veiled by snow-covered hills and ancient oaks whose branches twist and arch to form a living gateway. Those who seek the forest must do so with a pure heart, guided by the soft, ethereal glow of moonlight on the snow.

As you step through the entrance, a hush falls around you. The air grows colder, yet strangely comforting, filled with the scents of pine, cinnamon, and crisp winter. Snowflakes drift gently from the sky, sparkling like stars against the dark canopy above. It is here, among the towering pines and frosted ferns, that the creatures of Christmas make their home.

The Guardians of the Forest: Santa's Reindeer

Deeper into the forest, near a grove of ancient evergreens, you might catch a glimpse of the most noble inhabitants of this magical realm—Santa's reindeer. Sleek and majestic, these reindeer are unlike any found in the ordinary world. Their coats shimmer with a silver hue, and when they run, the ground beneath their hooves seems to glow, leaving trails of stardust on the snow.

Each reindeer has a name and a personality, known not only for their flying prowess but also for their roles as protectors of the forest. They possess a deep bond with the land, able to sense the forest's magic and guide lost travelers back to safety.

The Legend of Rudolph:

Rudolph, the most famous of Santa's reindeer, did not always have his glowing red nose. The legend tells of a time when a fierce blizzard threatened to cloak the world in darkness on Christmas Eve. As Santa prepared for his journey, he found himself unable to navigate through the storm's thick fog. It was then that Rudolph, a young and shy reindeer with a peculiar glowing nose, stepped forward. With courage and kindness in his heart, he led the way through the storm, his nose shining brightly like a beacon. From that night on, Rudolph became the forest's guiding light, symbolizing hope and the belief that even the smallest among us can shine the brightest.

The Tree Spirits: The Yule Sprites

In the heart of the forest grows the Grand Yule Tree, an immense evergreen whose branches stretch wide, adorned with ornaments crafted by nature itself—icicles, pinecones, and frost-kissed berries. This tree is home to the Yule Sprites, tiny, luminous beings with wings like dragonflies and laughter like the tinkling of bells.

The Yule Sprites are the forest's caretakers, tending to the trees and ensuring that the forest remains evergreen throughout the winter. They are responsible for weaving the intricate patterns of frost that appear on windows each morning and for coaxing the trees to release their piney scent into the air. The sprites also have a penchant for decorating, adding a touch of magic to everything they touch, from the forest floor to the stars in the sky.

The Tale of the Yule Star:

According to forest lore, it is the Yule Sprites who place the star atop the Grand Yule Tree each Christmas Eve. The star is said to be made of pure starlight, a gift from the celestial beings who watch over the world. It shines so brightly that its light can be seen from the farthest reaches of the forest, guiding creatures back to their homes and reminding them that the spirit of Christmas is a beacon of hope and unity.

The Tricksters: The Christmas Elves

No forest of Christmas would be complete without the mischievous presence of the Christmas elves. These playful creatures are known for their boundless energy, creativity, and penchant for pranks. They live in small, mushroom-shaped cottages scattered throughout the forest, their rooftops dusted with sugar-like snow.

During the year, the elves work diligently to create the toys and gifts that Santa delivers to children on Christmas Eve. However, their real joy comes from the mischief they weave into their creations. They are the reason wind-up toys sometimes whirl off course and why jack-in-the-boxes spring out with an extra bounce. The elves' laughter fills the forest as they test each toy, ensuring that it brings delight and surprise.

The Legend of the Wish Stones:

Hidden within the forest are the magical *Wish Stones*, small, iridescent pebbles that are said to grant a single wish to those who find them. Legend has it that the elves, with their curious nature, discovered these stones long ago. Rather than using the stones for themselves, they decided to hide them throughout the forest, allowing only those who are truly in need to stumble upon them. Thus, it is said that those who wander the forest with an open heart may find a Wish Stone and have their most cherished wish granted by the spirit of Christmas.

The Forest Protectors: The Nutcracker Soldiers

Standing tall and steadfast among the snowy glades are the Nutcracker Soldiers, guardians of the forest. They are made of carved wood, painted with bright colors, and adorned with brass buttons and feathered hats. At first glance, they appear as mere statues, their expressions stern and unchanging. However, on Christmas Eve, they come to life, patrolling the forest's borders to keep it safe from any who would seek to harm its magic.

The Nutcrackers hold a special bond with the creatures of the forest, particularly the woodland animals that gather around them for protection. They are known for their bravery and sense of honor, and their wooden hearts beat with the rhythm of the forest itself.

The Battle of the Sugarplum Grove:

One of the oldest tales told among the Nutcrackers is the *Battle of the Sugarplum Grove*. Long ago, a dark spirit of winter sought to steal the forest's magic by capturing the grove where the sweetest fruits and berries grew. The Nutcracker Soldiers rallied to protect the grove, wielding candy canes and gingerbread shields. With the help of the Yule Sprites, they repelled the dark spirit, ensuring that the forest's magic remained pure. To this day, the Sugarplum Grove stands as a testament to the courage and unity of the forest's protectors.

The Mystical Creatures: The Snow Hares and Ice Foxes

Among the forest's inhabitants are creatures touched by Christmas magic. The snow hares, with their gleaming white fur and eyes like polished silver, are known for their speed and agility. They dart through the forest like gusts of wind, leaving behind trails of sparkling snow. These hares are said to be messengers of the winter spirits, carrying news of the season's arrival to every corner of the forest.

Then there are the ice foxes, elegant and elusive, their coats shimmering with shades of blue and silver. They are the keepers of the forest's secrets, moving silently through the snow, their eyes reflecting the wisdom of ages. It is believed that if you encounter an ice fox and whisper a wish into its ear, it will carry that wish to the Yule Star, where it may come true.

The Fox's Promise:

A tale often shared among the forest's creatures is that of *The Fox's Promise*. The story goes that a long time ago, a small boy wandered into the forest on a cold, starless night. Lost and frightened, he stumbled upon an ice fox sitting gracefully under a pine tree. The fox, sensing the boy's despair, promised to guide him back to the village. With each step, the fox's fur glowed softly, lighting their path through the darkness. When they reached the forest's edge, the boy whispered his gratitude, and the fox replied, "Your kindness has warmed the forest's heart. Remember, the spirit of Christmas is found in the light you carry within." From that day forward, the boy became a protector of the forest, reminding all who entered to tread with care and love.

The Heart of the Forest: The Mistletoe Glade

In the center of the Enchanted Forest lies a hidden glade where mistletoe grows in abundance. Unlike the mistletoe found in the ordinary world, these plants have leaves that shimmer with a golden hue and berries that glow softly in the moonlight. The glade is a place of peace and love, where the magic of Christmas is at its most potent.

It is here that the forest's creatures gather on Christmas Eve for the *Mistletoe Feast*, a celebration of unity, friendship, and the joy of the season. The Yule Sprites weave garlands of mistletoe, which the reindeer hang from the branches above, creating a canopy of light and warmth. The Nutcracker Soldiers stand guard, while the elves serve platters of sugared fruits, gingerbread, and hot spiced cider.

The Mistletoe Wish:

The highlight of the Mistletoe Feast is the tradition of the *Mistletoe Wish*. As the feast draws to a close, each creature places a sprig of mistletoe at the base of the Grand Yule Tree and makes a silent wish for the coming year. It is believed that the tree's magic amplifies these wishes, spreading goodwill and blessings throughout the forest and beyond. The tradition reminds all who dwell in the forest that Christmas is a time for hope, kindness, and the belief in a world filled with love.

The Spirit of the Enchanted Forest

The Enchanted Forest is more than just a place of legend; it is a reflection of the magic that lies within the heart of Christmas itself. It teaches us that the season is not only about gifts and festivities but also about the joy of giving, the courage to hope, and the warmth of friendship. As you journey through its mythical paths and encounter its wondrous creatures, may you carry a piece of its enchantment with you, sharing the light of the forest with those around you.

And should you ever find yourself wandering in a snow-covered wood on a quiet winter's night, keep your eyes open for the glimmer of starlight on the snow. You may just stumble upon the entrance to the Enchanted Forest, where the spirit of Christmas awaits with open arms, ready to fill your heart with its timeless magic.

Chapter 17: Reindeer Legends

Santa's reindeer are some of the most cherished symbols of Christmas, their names instantly evoking the magic and wonder of the season. These magnificent creatures are more than mere animals; they are mythic beings imbued with the spirit of the winter sky, known for their strength, grace, and ability to fly across the world in a single night. The origins of Santa's reindeer are steeped in magical legends that have been told for centuries, each tale adding to their mystical allure. This chapter delves into the mythical roots of Santa's reindeer and unfolds a whimsical story of a young reindeer's first flight, highlighting the courage, excitement, and enchantment of joining Santa's legendary team.

The Magical Origins of Santa's Reindeer

The lore surrounding Santa's reindeer dates back to ancient times, long before they were first named in the 1823 poem "A Visit from St. Nicholas" (commonly known as "The Night Before Christmas"). The concept of flying reindeer is believed to have evolved from a blend of cultural myths, folklore, and the natural majesty of real-life reindeer that thrive in the Arctic's snowy realms.

1. Norse and Sami Myths

One possible origin of Santa's reindeer lies in Norse mythology. The reindeer were sacred to the Norse gods, particularly to the goddess Frigg, the goddess of motherhood, fertility, and winter. It was believed that reindeer could traverse the realms of the gods, riding the skies during the long, dark winter nights. In this lore, reindeer were not only swift but also wise, capable of navigating the treacherous Arctic weather through their connection with the stars and northern lights.

The indigenous Sami people of northern Scandinavia have also long revered reindeer. For them, reindeer symbolize survival, abundance, and the harmony between humans and nature. They believed that reindeer possessed a mystical energy, especially during the winter solstice, when the boundaries between the physical world and the spirit world became thin. It is said that Sami shamans could communicate with the reindeer spirits, seeking guidance and blessings for the coming year.

2. The Northern Lights and Reindeer Flight

The idea of flying reindeer is closely linked to the phenomena of the northern lights, or *aurora borealis*. In Finnish and Norse folklore, the northern lights were thought to be the glimmering path of magical reindeer as they danced across the sky. The lights were seen as a mystical energy that connected the earth to the heavens, and the reindeer, being creatures of both realms, could tap into this power to fly.

Legends say that Santa's reindeer are chosen for their unique bond with the aurora. Born during a northern lights display, they are imbued with stardust, granting them their extraordinary abilities. When they run, their hooves generate a spark of light that, when combined with the magic of Christmas Eve, allows them to lift off the ground and fly through the night sky.

3. The Naming of Santa's Reindeer

The first official naming of Santa's reindeer appeared in the 1823 poem "A Visit from St. Nicholas." The poem described eight reindeer: Dasher, Dancer, Prancer, Vixen, Comet, Cupid, Donder (now known as Donner), and Blitzen. Each name was carefully chosen to reflect the qualities of these magical creatures:

- **Dasher**: Known for his incredible speed, Dasher represents the swiftness and agility of the reindeer team.
- **Dancer**: Graceful and lively, Dancer embodies the joy and spirit of the season, moving effortlessly through the air.
- **Prancer**: Elegant and proud, Prancer's leaps are a sight to behold, showcasing the beauty of Christmas magic.
- **Vixen**: Clever and spirited, Vixen is often the spark of mischief among the reindeer, her wit as sharp as a winter wind.
- **Comet**: Named after the celestial phenomena, Comet is known for his bright, guiding presence, leading the way through the darkest nights.

- **Cupid**: The embodiment of love and warmth, Cupid's charm keeps the reindeer team unified and spirited throughout their journey.
- **Donner (originally Donder)**: With a name meaning "thunder," Donner brings strength and power, echoing the sound of his hooves like distant thunder across the sky.
- **Blitzen**: Meaning "lightning," Blitzen is the reindeer of speed and energy, his movements electrifying and swift.

Of course, the most famous reindeer of all—Rudolph—joined the team later in the 20th century, becoming a beloved symbol of courage and individuality. His tale reminds us that even the most unexpected among us can shine brightly and guide others through the darkest times.

The Whimsical Story: A Young Reindeer's First Flight

The Enchanted Forest had long been abuzz with excitement as Christmas approached. Snow dusted the ancient pines, and the northern lights flickered softly above, casting hues of green, pink, and blue across the twilight sky. In a clearing near Santa's stables, the young reindeer eagerly awaited their chance to prove themselves for the honor of joining Santa's legendary team.

Among them stood **Liora**, a small, doe-eyed reindeer with a glossy, chestnut coat. Liora had been dreaming of this moment since she was a fawn. She had listened to the tales of Dasher's speed, Comet's guiding light, and Rudolph's heroic flight through the stormy Christmas Eve. She had trained tirelessly, practicing her leaps and learning to navigate by the stars, hoping that one day she might earn her place among the legendary reindeer.

Today was the day. Santa's head reindeer, Donner, stood before the young hopefuls, his voice booming like the thunder he was named after. "Listen well," he began. "Tonight, each of you will have a chance to take to the skies. Remember, flight is not just about strength or speed—it's about heart and the magic that lies within you. Open yourself to the enchantment of the northern lights, and they will lift you up."

Liora's heart raced as Donner spoke. She felt a mixture of excitement and nerves. Could she truly fly? She closed her eyes and took a deep breath, feeling the crisp, cold air fill her lungs. She had to try.

The young reindeer lined up in the clearing, each taking turns to make their attempt. Some leaped confidently, while others stumbled. As Liora's turn approached, she felt a flutter in her chest—a blend of fear and exhilaration.

"Ready, Liora?" Donner asked, his eyes warm with encouragement.

"Yes," she replied, her voice steady. She took a deep breath and fixed her gaze on the horizon, where the northern lights danced in the sky.

Liora started to run, her hooves digging into the snow-covered ground. The forest blurred around her, and for a moment, she felt a rush of doubt. *What if I fall? What if I'm not ready?* But then, she remembered the stories of Rudolph and the others, and how they had overcome their own challenges. *Flight is about heart and magic,* she reminded herself.

As she approached the edge of the clearing, she pushed off with all her might, leaping into the air. For a heartbeat, she felt nothing but the icy wind rushing past her. But then, something incredible happened. A warmth spread through her, starting from her chest and flowing to the tips of her hooves. She looked down and gasped—the ground was far below, and she was soaring.

Liora laughed, a joyous, lighthearted sound that echoed through the forest. She tilted her head upwards and reached out to the northern lights, feeling their energy hum around her like a gentle embrace. She wasn't just flying; she was gliding, carried by the magic of the sky itself.

The other young reindeer watched in awe as Liora made her first flight. She twisted and twirled, her movements growing bolder and more graceful with each passing moment. When she finally landed, breathless and beaming, Donner approached her with a smile.

"Well done, Liora," he said, his voice filled with pride. "You have the heart and spirit of a true Christmas reindeer."

Liora's eyes shone with happiness as the other reindeer gathered around her, offering words of congratulations and admiration. She had done it. She had found the magic within herself and taken flight.

That night, as the stars sparkled above the forest and Santa prepared his sleigh for the Christmas journey, Liora stood with the other reindeer, ready to take her place among the legends. The northern lights shimmered in the sky, casting a warm glow over the clearing, as if to welcome her into their timeless dance.

As Santa approached and fastened the reins, he looked at Liora and smiled. "Tonight, you join the team," he said. "Remember, it's not just about delivering gifts. It's about bringing light and joy to the world. And that is a magic only a true reindeer of Christmas can share."

And so, Liora took her place beside Dasher, Dancer, and the others, her heart swelling with pride. As the sleigh lifted off and soared into the starry sky, she felt the magic of the season fill her, guiding her through the night. For Liora, this was not just her first flight—it was the beginning of a journey filled with wonder, joy, and the timeless spirit of Christmas.

The Enduring Magic of Santa's Reindeer

The legends of Santa's reindeer continue to inspire awe and wonder, reminding us of the magic that comes with the Christmas season. These noble creatures, with their unique names and qualities, symbolize the blend of strength, courage, joy, and love that the holiday brings. Each flight they make across the night sky is a testament to the belief that, with a bit of heart and a touch of magic, we can soar to great heights and bring light to the world around us.

So, the next time you look up at the sky on Christmas Eve, keep an eye out for a flash of light or a gleaming trail of stardust. You may just catch a glimpse of Santa's reindeer, led by the newest young flier, as they race across the heavens, carrying the magic of Christmas to every corner of the earth.

Chapter 18: The Secret of Snowflakes

There is something inherently magical about snow. When the first flakes begin to fall, it feels as if the world is being transformed into a glistening wonderland. Each snowflake, delicate and unique, is a tiny marvel of nature's artistry. But beyond their ethereal beauty, snowflakes hold secrets both scientific and mystical. In this chapter, we will explore the science behind snowflake formation and delve into the folklore and magic that snow has inspired throughout history. Alongside this exploration, you'll find instructions for creating snow-inspired crafts to bring a touch of winter's enchantment into your home.

The Science of Snowflakes: Nature's Frozen Art

Every snowflake begins its journey high in the atmosphere, formed from a simple droplet of water vapor. As the water vapor rises into the cold upper reaches of the atmosphere, it freezes onto a particle of dust or pollen, creating the initial ice crystal. This small crystal becomes the seed from which the snowflake will grow, as more water vapor condenses and freezes onto its surface. The crystal starts to develop intricate, symmetrical patterns, influenced by factors such as temperature, humidity, and air currents.

1. The Structure of a Snowflake: Six-Sided Symmetry

One of the most fascinating aspects of snowflakes is their six-sided (hexagonal) symmetry. This symmetry arises from the molecular structure of water. When water molecules freeze, they naturally arrange themselves into a hexagonal lattice, resulting in six evenly spaced branches. As the snowflake falls through varying atmospheric conditions, each of its six branches grows in a similar pattern, giving the snowflake its characteristic, symmetrical beauty.

2. Why No Two Snowflakes Are Alike

The phrase "no two snowflakes are alike" is rooted in truth. As a snowflake tumbles through the atmosphere, it encounters different temperatures and humidity levels, which affect its growth. The branches of the snowflake grow at slightly different rates, influenced by minute changes in their environment. This means that each snowflake develops a unique pattern, with its shape and design determined by the journey it takes from the sky to the ground. With countless variations in atmospheric conditions, the chances of two snowflakes forming exactly the same structure are extraordinarily slim.

3. Types of Snowflakes: Stars, Plates, and Columns

Not all snowflakes have the classic star-like shape. In fact, snowflakes can form in a variety of shapes, depending on the temperature and humidity at which they crystallize. The main types include:

- **Stellar Dendrites:** The classic star-shaped snowflakes with six intricate branches. They form in cold temperatures with high humidity, resulting in their elaborate and delicate patterns.
- **Plates:** Thin, flat snowflakes that resemble hexagonal plates. They form at slightly warmer temperatures, often displaying simple, symmetrical shapes.
- **Columns:** These snowflakes take the form of small, hexagonal columns or needles. They typically form in colder, drier conditions and may cluster together to create more complex shapes.
- **Capped Columns:** A unique type of snowflake that forms when columnar snowflakes encounter different conditions and grow small plate-like extensions at their ends, creating a capped appearance.

The Magic of Snow in Folklore and Mythology

Throughout history, snow has been a source of inspiration, wonder, and even reverence. Many cultures have woven stories and beliefs around snow, attributing mystical properties to its beauty and power.

1. Snow as a Symbol of Purity and Renewal

In many cultures, snow is seen as a symbol of purity, blanketing the earth in a fresh, white layer that covers all blemishes and imperfections. This symbolism is closely tied to the idea of renewal. As snow falls, it marks the end of the old and the preparation for the new—a quiet pause in nature that precedes the rebirth of spring. In this sense, snow represents both a cleansing force and a promise of new beginnings.

2. The Spirit of the Snow Maiden

In Eastern European folklore, the *Snow Maiden* (*Snegurochka* in Russian) is a mystical figure associated with winter. She is said to be made of snow and ice, with hair as white as frost and eyes as blue as the sky. The Snow Maiden is both beautiful and ethereal, embodying the fleeting and fragile nature of winter. According to legend, she can only exist while the snow remains; when spring arrives, she melts away, returning to the realm of winter spirits. Stories of the Snow Maiden highlight the delicate beauty of snow and the bittersweet passage of the seasons.

3. The Magic of Snowflakes in Spells and Charms

In various folk traditions, snowflakes have been used in magical practices. They are believed to capture the essence of winter's stillness and clarity. In some cultures, it was said that catching a snowflake on your tongue could bring good luck for the coming year, as it was thought to grant a brief taste of nature's purity. Similarly, carrying a snowflake-shaped charm was believed to invoke the protection and tranquility of winter.

Snow-Inspired Crafts: Bringing the Enchantment of Snow Indoors

Snowflakes may be fleeting, but their beauty can be captured in crafts that bring the magic of winter into your home. The following snow-inspired crafts are easy to make and perfect for adding a touch of snowy wonder to your holiday decor.

1. Crystal Snowflakes

Create your own sparkling snowflakes using simple household materials. These crystal snowflakes are not only beautiful but also a fun science experiment that demonstrates how crystals form.

Materials Needed:

- White pipe cleaners
- Scissors
- String
- Pencil or chopstick
- Wide-mouth glass jar
- Borax powder
- Boiling water
- Food coloring (optional)

Instructions:

1. Cut the pipe cleaners into three equal pieces. Twist them together at the center to form a six-pointed star shape, resembling a snowflake. You can add smaller pieces to the ends to create more intricate designs.
2. Tie a piece of string to one of the points of the snowflake and then tie the other end of the string to a pencil or chopstick.
3. Fill the glass jar with boiling water, leaving a little space at the top. Add borax powder, one tablespoon at a time, stirring until it dis-

solves. You'll need about three tablespoons of borax for each cup of water. If you want colored snowflakes, add a few drops of food coloring.

4. Lower the snowflake into the jar, ensuring it is completely submerged and not touching the sides or bottom. Rest the pencil across the top of the jar.

5. Leave the jar in a cool, undisturbed place overnight. As the water cools, borax crystals will form on the pipe cleaner snowflake.

6. Carefully remove the snowflake from the jar and let it dry. Hang it in a window or on a tree to catch the light and sparkle like real snow.

Magical Element: Just as real snowflakes crystallize in the sky, these pipe cleaner snowflakes will grow their own unique crystals, bringing the beauty of winter indoors.

2. Paper Snowflake Garlands

Paper snowflakes are a classic craft that captures the intricate patterns of real snowflakes. By stringing them together, you can create a beautiful garland to adorn windows, walls, or mantels.

Materials Needed:

- White paper (printer paper, tissue paper, or coffee filters work well)
- Scissors
- String or yarn
- Tape

Instructions:

1. Start by cutting a square piece of paper. Fold it in half diagonally to form a triangle.
2. Fold the triangle in half again, then fold it into thirds, overlapping the edges. You should now have a small, wedge-shaped piece.
3. Use scissors to cut shapes along the edges of the folded paper. Get creative with your cuts; try triangles, circles, or wavy lines to create different patterns.
4. Carefully unfold the paper to reveal your snowflake. Repeat the process to make multiple snowflakes.
5. Attach the snowflakes to a piece of string using tape, spacing them evenly to create a garland.
6. Hang the garland across a window, doorframe, or mantel for a touch of winter magic.

Magical Element: Each paper snowflake is unique, just like those that fall from the sky. Hanging them in your home creates a whimsical winter wonderland.

3. Snowball Bath Bombs

Capture the essence of a snowball in a luxurious bath bomb, perfect for gifting or enjoying yourself. These fizzy, moisturizing bath bombs will dissolve in water, releasing soothing scents and nourishing ingredients.

Materials Needed:

- 1 cup baking soda
- 1/2 cup citric acid
- 1/2 cup Epsom salts
- 1/2 cup cornstarch
- 2 tablespoons coconut oil, melted
- 1 teaspoon vanilla extract or essential oil (for scent)
- Water (in a spray bottle)
- Mixing bowl
- Snowball mold (or any round mold)

Instructions:

1. In a mixing bowl, combine the baking soda, citric acid, Epsom salts, and cornstarch. Stir until evenly mixed.
2. Add the melted coconut oil and vanilla extract or essential oil. Mix thoroughly. The mixture will be crumbly at this stage.
3. Using a spray bottle, lightly mist the mixture with water, stirring continuously. Be careful not to add too much water, as the mixture may start to fizz. It should begin to hold its shape when pressed together.
4. Press the mixture firmly into your mold. If using a snowball mold, pack both halves tightly and press them together.

5. Let the bath bombs dry for at least 24 hours. Carefully remove them from the molds and store in an airtight container until ready to use.

Magical Element: These snowball bath bombs bring the magic of a winter snowfall into your bath. As they fizz and dissolve, they release soothing scents and moisturizing oils, turning your bath into a relaxing, snow-inspired retreat.

4. Snowy Candle Holders

Create a cozy, snowy ambiance with frosted candle holders. These candle holders, dusted with Epsom salts, mimic the glistening surface of freshly fallen snow.

Materials Needed:

- Glass candle holders or jars
- Mod Podge or white glue
- Epsom salts
- Paintbrush

Instructions:

1. Clean the glass candle holders and dry them thoroughly.
2. Use a paintbrush to apply an even layer of Mod Podge or white glue on the outside of each candle holder.
3. While the glue is still wet, sprinkle Epsom salts over the surface, covering it entirely. The salts will stick to the glue, creating a frosted, snowy texture.
4. Allow the candle holders to dry completely before using.
5. Place a tea light or small candle inside each holder. When lit, the candle will glow through the frosted glass, casting a warm, wintry light.

Magical Element: The frosted candle holders bring the beauty of snow indoors, illuminating your space with a soft, enchanting glow reminiscent of a winter night.

The Magic of Snow at Home

The beauty and wonder of snow lie not only in its physical form but also in the sense of magic and tranquility it brings. Whether you are marveling at the science of snowflake formation, embracing the folklore of snow spirits, or crafting snow-inspired decor, you are connecting with the timeless enchantment of winter. These crafts allow you to capture a piece of that magic and bring it into your home, creating an atmosphere of warmth, peace, and wonder.

As you create your snow-inspired crafts, remember the intricate journey each real snowflake takes to become what it is. Let them remind you of the beauty in fleeting moments and the unique paths that shape who we are. By celebrating the secrets of snowflakes, you not only honor nature's artistry but also invite the quiet magic of winter to become a part of your holiday season.

Chapter 19: Frost Fairy Tales

Winter nights have a special kind of magic. As temperatures drop and the world becomes cloaked in a blanket of snow, the frost fairies come out to dance. These elusive creatures of winter weave their icy spells, transforming landscapes with glistening patterns and sparkling crystals. Their tales have been whispered through generations, stories of beauty, mischief, and the quiet power of nature. In this chapter, you'll find a collection of short fairy tales that delve into the lives of these frost fairies, revealing how they bring the magic of winter to life.

1. The Frost Queen and the Frozen Lake

Once upon a time, deep within a winter forest, there was a lake so still and clear that it mirrored the sky perfectly. In the heart of this forest lived the Frost Queen, the eldest and most powerful of the frost fairies. Her touch could freeze rivers and turn morning dew into delicate crystals. She had long silvery hair that sparkled like fresh snow, and her eyes gleamed with the light of a thousand frosty mornings.

Each year, as winter approached, it was the Frost Queen's duty to blanket the forest with frost. But this year, something troubled her. The lake, which had always been her pride and joy, refused to freeze. No matter how many icy spells she cast, the water remained clear, reflecting the stars and moon with an ethereal glow.

"Why do you resist the frost, my dear lake?" she murmured, kneeling by its edge. The lake only rippled softly in response.

Days turned to weeks, and the Frost Queen's concern grew. The lake needed to freeze, for it was the heart of the forest's winter magic. Without its frozen surface, the frost would not spread as it should, leaving the forest vulnerable to the harshness of the cold.

In her worry, the Frost Queen summoned the younger frost fairies. They gathered around the lake, their wings shimmering in the pale light of the moon.

"We must find a way to help the lake freeze," she told them. "Lend me your magic, and perhaps together, we can uncover the secret that binds it."

The frost fairies circled the lake, their delicate hands glowing with icy blue light. They whispered ancient chants, drawing patterns in the air. Slowly, a mist began to rise from the water, swirling and coiling until it formed the shape of a figure—a spirit of the lake.

"Why do you wish to freeze me?" asked the spirit, its voice like the sound of a distant stream. "I have no quarrel with winter, but I am bound by a promise made long ago."

The Frost Queen approached, her expression one of concern and curiosity. "What promise do you speak of, spirit?"

The spirit sighed, and the air grew colder. "A young girl came here last spring, seeking refuge from sorrow. She wept by my shore, and I vowed to remain unfrozen until her heart was healed. She has not returned, and so I keep my promise, holding back the frost."

The Frost Queen thought for a moment, understanding the depth of the lake's loyalty. "Then we shall help her," she said. "For only when the heart is warmed by hope can the winter magic flow freely."

She called upon the forest's magic, sending a gentle wind to find the girl. The wind traveled far, carrying whispers of the lake's plight to the ears of the one who had sought its comfort.

When the girl returned, her eyes were filled with tears, but also a glimmer of understanding. She knelt by the lake, placing her hands upon its surface. "Thank you for holding my sorrow," she whispered. "But now, I am ready to let it go."

As she spoke, a warmth spread through the water. The spirit of the lake sighed in relief, and a thin layer of frost began to form on its surface. The Frost Queen and her fairies watched in awe as the lake transformed, freezing into a sheet of shimmering ice.

From that day on, the lake and the girl shared a special bond. The Frost Queen, with her fairies, cast their frosty magic across the forest, bringing winter's beauty in full force. And each year, when winter arrived, the girl would return to the lake, standing by its frozen edge, grateful for the frost fairies' help in warming her heart.

2. The Ice Flower and the Curious Fairy

In a quiet glade where snow lay thick upon the ground, there grew an ice flower—rare and beautiful. Its petals were crystalline, reflecting the moonlight in a kaleidoscope of colors. The flower was tended by a small frost fairy named Eira, whose curiosity often led her into trouble.

Eira had been assigned to guard the ice flower, for it was the source of the forest's frost magic. Each winter, its bloom would signal the arrival of the frost fairies, allowing them to spread their icy patterns across the land. But Eira found herself drawn to the flower's mysteries, wondering how it could remain so vibrant amidst the cold.

One night, as the stars twinkled overhead, Eira decided to discover the flower's secret. "If I can understand how it blooms in winter," she mused, "perhaps I can create more ice flowers and fill the forest with beauty."

With delicate hands, she reached out to touch the flower's petals. At her touch, the flower glowed with a soft light, warming her fingertips. Suddenly, the petals began to curl inward, and the flower's glow dimmed. Eira gasped, realizing that she had disturbed its magic.

"Oh no," she whispered, her heart pounding. "What have I done?"

The glade grew colder as the ice flower wilted, its petals losing their luster. Without the ice flower's bloom, the frost magic would weaken, leaving the forest vulnerable. Eira felt tears welling up in her eyes, knowing that she had let her curiosity lead her astray.

Just then, an older frost fairy named Astrid appeared. Her wings shimmered with an ancient light, and her gaze was both stern and kind.

"You touched the flower without understanding its magic," she said gently. "But there is still hope."

Eira looked up, her eyes pleading. "Can we save it? I didn't mean to harm it, I just wanted to understand."

Astrid nodded. "The ice flower blooms because of the balance between warmth and cold. To revive it, you must give it a piece of your own warmth—a gesture of care and selflessness."

Eira took a deep breath, feeling the weight of her mistake. She knelt by the wilted flower and placed her hands upon the ground. Closing her eyes, she concentrated on the warmth within her heart—the love for the forest, the joy of winter's beauty. Slowly, a soft glow spread from her hands into the earth.

The ice flower trembled, its petals unfurling as a gentle frost covered them once more. It began to glow with renewed light, brighter than before, reflecting Eira's warmth and the love she had given to restore it.

The glade filled with frost once more, and the winter magic flowed through the forest. Eira stood, her heart filled with gratitude and newfound understanding. She had learned that some mysteries are not meant to be unraveled by force, but by the patience and care that come from a place of love.

From that night on, Eira guarded the ice flower with a humble heart, sharing its beauty with the forest without seeking to possess its secrets. And each winter, when the ice flower bloomed, the glade would sparkle with colors as a reminder of the curious fairy who had learned the true magic of balance and care.

3. The Frost Painter and the Starlit Garden

At the edge of the northern forest, where the trees met the sky, lived a frost fairy named Aislin. She was known as the Frost Painter, for it was her duty to create the frost patterns that adorned windows, leaves, and streams. Aislin had a talent for crafting intricate designs, swirling spirals, and delicate branches that captured the wonder of winter.

One evening, as Aislin worked on a frozen pond, she noticed something unusual—a star had fallen from the sky and lay nestled among the reeds. Its light was faint, but it pulsed with an ethereal glow.

Aislin approached the star, her eyes wide with awe. "You've fallen so far," she murmured, gently cradling it in her hands. "I must find a way to help you."

The star flickered, its light dimming further. Aislin felt a pang of worry. The star needed a place to recover, to gather its strength and return to the sky. But where could she take it?

Then an idea struck her. "The Starlit Garden," she whispered. "If I plant you there, perhaps you can regain your light."

The Starlit Garden was a hidden place deep within the forest, where frost fairies went to meditate and restore their magic. It was said that the garden's frost flowers absorbed the light of the stars, allowing them to bloom even in the darkest nights.

With the star in her hands, Aislin flew through the forest, her wings leaving trails of sparkling frost behind her. She reached the garden, its snowy landscape dotted with faintly glowing flowers. Carefully, she knelt and placed the star in the center of the garden.

The ground shimmered, and the frost flowers leaned toward the star, sharing their light. Slowly, the star began to glow brighter, its light mingling with the frost and illuminating the garden in a soft, magical glow.

Aislin watched in wonder as the star lifted itself from the ground, its light growing ever stronger. It rose into the sky, joining its brethren among the stars, shining with a renewed brilliance.

As the garden basked in the star's glow, Aislin felt a deep sense of joy and fulfillment. She had given the star a place to recover, and in turn, it had filled the garden with light.

From that night on, the Starlit Garden became known as a place where fallen stars could find refuge, tended by the frost fairies who understood the magic of giving and the beauty of restoration.

The Magic of the Frost Fairies

The frost fairies bring more than just cold and frost to the world; they bring stories of compassion, balance, and wonder. Their delicate patterns on windows, the glittering snowflakes, and the quiet beauty of a frozen landscape all speak of their presence. These tales remind us that even in the coldest season, there is warmth to be found in acts of kindness, curiosity, and the simple appreciation of nature's fleeting wonders.

As you walk through a frosty morning, or see the delicate etchings of ice on a window, remember the frost fairies and their tales. They are the silent artists of winter, each one painting their own story in the canvas of the season. Their magic is not just in the frost they create, but in the gentle lessons they leave behind—lessons of care, balance, and the quiet strength found in the beauty of the cold.

Chapter 20: The Crystal Lake

In the farthest reaches of the winter forest, nestled among ancient pines and guarded by towering mountains, lies a frozen expanse of breathtaking beauty known as the *Crystal Lake.* No ordinary lake, this body of water is the subject of legends passed down through generations, stories that speak of its mystical powers and the miracles it brings to those who dare to seek it. The lake is said to grant Christmas wishes, but only to those who possess a heart of pure intention. This is the tale of the Crystal Lake, its magic, and a young girl's quest to uncover the truth of its legend.

The Legend of the Crystal Lake

Long ago, when the world was young, the winter spirits gathered to create a place where their magic could dwell undisturbed. They chose a secluded valley surrounded by mountains and forests, a place where silence and serenity reigned. There, they shaped a lake, its waters so clear that they reflected the sky with perfect clarity. As a final blessing, the winter spirits breathed their magic into the lake, turning its waters into a frozen mirror that glistened like crystal under the light of the stars.

It was then that the lake gained its power: to grant wishes on Christmas Eve. But the magic was bound by a rule—the wish could only be granted to those whose hearts were pure, free of greed, envy, or malice. The lake would open its secrets to those who came with hope, love, and the desire to share joy with others.

Over the centuries, many have ventured to the Crystal Lake, drawn by its legend. Some left with nothing, their hearts weighed down by desires that the lake could not fulfill. But others, those who sought not for themselves but for the happiness of others, found their wishes answered in ways that changed their lives forever.

The Journey to the Crystal Lake: A Story of Hope

This tale begins in a small village, nestled at the edge of the great winter forest. The villagers lived simple lives, finding joy in the quiet beauty of nature and the warmth of their community. But one winter, a deep sadness fell over the village. The crops had failed that year, and many families faced a difficult winter with little food and warmth. Despite the villagers' best efforts, worry and despair settled over the once-merry community.

In this village lived a young girl named Elara. She was known for her kind heart and hopeful spirit, always bringing a smile to those around her, even in the darkest of times. As Christmas approached, Elara watched her neighbors struggle to find joy in the season. The sight of their worry tugged at her heart, and she knew she had to do something.

One evening, as Elara sat by the fire with her grandmother, she spoke of her wish. "I wish I could bring joy back to the village, Grandmother," she said, her eyes reflecting the flickering flames. "But I don't know how."

Her grandmother, a wise woman with stories of old, looked at her thoughtfully. "There is a way, my dear," she said softly. "You have heard the legend of the Crystal Lake, have you not?"

Elara nodded. "The lake that grants wishes to those pure of heart. But it's just a story... isn't it?"

The grandmother smiled gently. "Legends often have roots in truth. The Crystal Lake lies deep within the forest, far from here. It is said that on Christmas Eve, the lake opens its magic to those who seek not for themselves but for the good of others. If you truly wish to help the village, you may find the lake and make your wish."

Elara's heart swelled with determination. She would find the Crystal Lake, no matter how far or difficult the journey. That night, as the village slept, she packed a small bag with food and warm clothing, wrapped a scarf around her neck, and set out into the forest under the light of the full moon.

The Journey Through the Winter Forest

The forest was vast and quiet, its trees standing tall like silent sentinels guarding ancient secrets. Snow crunched under Elara's boots as she made her way through the winding paths, guided by the silver glow of the moon. The air was crisp and cold, and the stars overhead twinkled brightly, as if watching over her journey.

Hours passed, and the forest grew darker. The path became more difficult, filled with snowdrifts and tangled roots. But Elara pressed on, her heart driven by the thought of bringing joy to her village. Just as fatigue began to set in, she stumbled upon a small clearing. In the center stood an ancient oak tree, its branches adorned with icicles that glistened like crystals.

As Elara approached, she noticed a faint shimmer in the air around the tree. From the shadows emerged a figure—an elderly man with a beard as white as snow and eyes that gleamed like frost. He was draped in a cloak of winter leaves, and his presence filled the air with a sense of magic.

"You seek the Crystal Lake," the man said, his voice deep and resonant. "But tell me, child, what is it that you truly wish for?"

Elara hesitated, feeling the weight of his gaze. She knew this was a test, a moment of truth that would reveal her heart's intention. "I wish for my village to find joy again," she replied, her voice steady. "Not for myself, but for everyone. They have lost hope, and I want to bring it back to them."

The man's eyes softened, and he nodded. "Your heart is pure, and your wish is selfless. Continue on this path, and you shall find what you seek."

With a wave of his hand, the path ahead of her glowed faintly, revealing a trail that wound deeper into the forest. Elara bowed her head in gratitude and continued her journey, following the illuminated path that led her closer to the lake.

The Crystal Lake Revealed

After hours of walking, just as dawn began to break on Christmas Eve, Elara emerged from the trees and gasped. Before her stretched the Crystal Lake, its surface frozen into a perfect, shimmering mirror that reflected the pale light of the morning sky. The lake was surrounded by snow-covered pines, their branches dusted with frost, creating a scene of serene beauty.

Elara approached the edge of the lake, her breath visible in the cold air. She felt a mixture of awe and trepidation, knowing that this was a moment of profound magic. Kneeling down, she placed her hands on the ice, feeling a gentle, tingling warmth spread through her fingertips.

"Great spirits of the lake," she whispered, her voice trembling with sincerity. "I come with a wish not for myself, but for my village. They have suffered much this winter, and I wish for their hearts to be filled with joy and hope once more."

For a moment, nothing happened. The lake remained still, its surface reflecting the trees and sky with perfect clarity. Then, slowly, a glow began to emanate from beneath the ice. The light grew brighter, spreading across the lake until it shone like a beacon, casting a soft, magical glow upon the entire clearing.

Elara watched in wonder as the light rose from the lake, forming a swirl of sparkling mist. It drifted upwards, transforming into countless tiny snowflakes that danced through the air before gently settling on the surrounding forest.

The mist encircled Elara, and she felt a warmth fill her heart, a sense of peace and fulfillment. The lake had heard her wish and granted it.

The Miracle of the Crystal Lake

With the magic released, Elara turned to make her way back to the village, her heart light and hopeful. As she walked, she noticed that the snow around her seemed to shimmer with an inner light, a sign of the lake's blessing spreading through the forest.

When Elara finally returned to her village, she found a scene of transformation. The once-gray skies had cleared, revealing a bright, crisp morning. Snow sparkled on the rooftops, and a sense of warmth emanated from every house. The villagers, who had awoken to this new day, stood outside in wonder.

"What happened?" they murmured among themselves. "It's as if the winter has brought us a miracle."

Elara approached her grandmother, her eyes shining with joy. "The legend is true," she said, her voice filled with wonder. "The Crystal Lake granted my wish."

From that day forward, the village found a renewed sense of joy and hope. Food and warmth seemed to come easier, and the people shared what they had with one another, their hearts filled with the spirit of giving. The story of Elara's journey spread, becoming a cherished tale of the village, passed down through generations as a reminder of the power of selflessness and the magic of the Crystal Lake.

The Enduring Magic of the Crystal Lake

The legend of the Crystal Lake endures, a story that speaks to the transformative power of pure-hearted wishes. It is said that each Christmas Eve, the lake opens its magic, granting wishes to those who come seeking not for themselves, but for the joy and well-being of others. The light that emerges from the lake spreads through the world, bringing warmth, love, and hope to all who need it.

And so, in the quiet of winter, when snow covers the earth and the air is filled with the stillness of the season, the Crystal Lake waits. It waits for those who carry the spirit of selfless love, ready to reveal its magic and grant wishes that come from the heart. Its legend reminds us that true magic lies not in what we gain for ourselves, but in what we give to others, creating a light that shines even in the coldest of winters.

Part 5: *Twilight Tales: Myths and Mysteries of Christmas Night*

Chapter 21: The Midnight Bells

Christmas Eve is a night steeped in magic and wonder, when the world seems to hold its breath in anticipation of something extraordinary. One of the oldest traditions is the ringing of bells at midnight, a practice that has endured through centuries and across cultures. It is said that when the clock strikes twelve, the bells toll not just to herald the arrival of Christmas but to unlock the hidden mysteries and enchantments of the season. In this chapter, we explore the legend of the *Midnight Bells* through a tale that intertwines magic, hope, and the mysteries of the heart.

The Legend of the Midnight Bells

Long ago, in a quaint village nestled at the foot of a great mountain, there stood an ancient stone church with a tall bell tower that reached toward the sky. Inside the tower hung a set of bells known as the *Midnight Bells*. Crafted by master bell-makers centuries earlier, each bell was inscribed with symbols and runes that spoke of hope, love, and the promise of miracles.

According to legend, the bells possessed a unique magic. When they rang at midnight on Christmas Eve, their chimes would resonate through the village, reaching into the hearts of those who listened with pure intent. It was said that during this moment, the world's secrets could be glimpsed, and wishes whispered to the bells would be heard by forces unknown. However, the magic of the Midnight Bells could only be unlocked once every hundred years, during the grand event known as the *Night of Secrets*.

The Village of Hartshollow and the Bells' Silence

In the village of Hartshollow, the Midnight Bells had long fallen silent. Many years had passed since they had last been rung at midnight. The villagers carried on with their Christmas traditions, but a shadow of old sorrows lingered over the community. Some whispered that the magic of the bells had been lost, while others believed that the village had simply forgotten how to listen to their chimes.

This year, however, was different. It was the hundredth year since the bells had last tolled for the Night of Secrets, and the air was thick with anticipation. There was a sense of restlessness in the village, a feeling that something wondrous was about to unfold. Yet, there was also fear, for it was rumored that the bells would only ring if they were given a reason to do so—something powerful enough to awaken their magic.

The Orphan and the Bells: The Story of Clare

In this village lived a young orphan girl named Clare. She was known for her kindness and bright spirit, despite the hardships she had faced. Clare lived at the edge of the village in a small cottage that had once belonged to her grandparents. Though her life was modest, she found joy in the simple things—reading books by candlelight, collecting pinecones in the forest, and listening to the stories of old that the village elders would share.

As Christmas approached, Clare could sense the unease in the village. People spoke of the Night of Secrets in hushed tones, uncertain if the Midnight Bells would ring and what it would mean if they did. Clare herself had grown up hearing the legend of the bells, how they could reveal secrets, grant wishes, or even bring a glimpse of magic into the world. Deep in her heart, she carried a wish—one she had never spoken aloud.

Clare's parents had passed away when she was very young, leaving her with a fragmentary memory of their love. On quiet nights, she would sometimes find herself gazing up at the bell tower, wondering if the bells could bring back the warmth of that love, even if just for a moment.

The Preparation for the Night of Secrets

As the days of December passed, the villagers began to prepare for Christmas. They decorated their homes with holly and ivy, hung lanterns on the streets, and baked sweet treats to share. Yet, the anticipation of the Night of Secrets loomed over everything. The village elders spoke of how, at midnight, they would gather around the church and listen for the bells.

"The bells will only ring if a heart pure enough to unlock their magic steps forward," one of the elders explained to the children, his eyes twinkling with mystery. "When they do, the secrets they hold will be revealed. But beware, for not all secrets are easy to hear."

Clare listened intently, feeling a flutter of excitement mixed with trepidation. Could she be the one to unlock the bells' magic? Her wish was simple, born from a deep yearning to feel connected to those she had lost. She decided that on Christmas Eve, she would go to the bell tower and offer her wish to the Midnight Bells.

Christmas Eve and the Approach of Midnight

Christmas Eve arrived, and a soft snowfall blanketed the village, casting a serene hush over the landscape. As the evening wore on, the villagers gathered at the church, their breath misting in the cold air. Inside, candles flickered, casting warm glows on the stone walls, while outside, the stars shone brightly in the clear, night sky.

Clare stood at the edge of the gathering, her heart pounding in her chest. Midnight was approaching, and the air was thick with an expectant stillness. The villagers watched the clock, their eyes fixed on the bell tower, hoping to hear the long-forgotten chimes.

With only a few minutes left until midnight, Clare took a deep breath and slipped away from the crowd. She made her way to the side of the church and climbed the narrow steps to the bell tower. As she ascended, the air grew colder, and a sense of ancient power seemed to thrum through the stones.

When she reached the top, she stood before the massive bells, their surfaces etched with symbols that glimmered faintly in the moonlight. Clare hesitated for a moment, feeling the weight of the legends pressing upon her. Then, she closed her eyes and placed her hands on the largest bell.

"I know you've been silent for so long," she whispered. "But I've come with a simple wish. I do not ask for riches or power, only to feel the love of my family once more. To know that they are still with me, even if I cannot see them."

She fell silent, her heart pounding in the stillness. The seconds stretched, and Clare feared that the bells would remain mute, that her wish was not enough to awaken their magic.

The Bells Ring Out: The Secrets Unlocked

Then, just as the clock struck midnight, a deep, resonant hum filled the air. Clare opened her eyes in shock as the bells began to tremble, their surfaces glowing with an inner light. The largest bell tolled first, its sound reverberating through the tower and echoing out into the night. One by one, the other bells joined in, their chimes creating a harmony that spread across the village like a wave.

The villagers below gasped, their faces alight with wonder. The Midnight Bells had rung! The sound wrapped around them, filling their hearts with warmth and bringing tears to their eyes. In that moment, they felt a surge of hope and magic that they had long forgotten.

Clare stood transfixed as the bells continued to chime. The air around her shimmered, and she saw faint, ethereal shapes forming in the light. She blinked, her breath catching in her throat. Before her appeared two figures—her parents, their faces kind and loving as she remembered. They smiled at her, their presence like a warm embrace that enveloped her in comfort and peace.

"Do not be afraid, Clare," her mother's voice echoed softly. "We have always been with you, in your heart and in the love you share with others."

Her father nodded. "The bells have revealed this truth to you. The magic of Christmas is in the love that transcends time and distance."

Tears streamed down Clare's face, but they were tears of joy. She felt the weight of her grief lift, replaced by a profound sense of connection. The vision of her parents slowly faded, leaving behind a feeling of warmth that settled into her very soul.

As the bells' final chime rang out, Clare knew that her wish had been granted—not in the way she had imagined, but in a way that filled her with hope and peace. The bells had revealed their secret: that love, once given, never truly disappears; it remains, woven into the fabric of our lives.

The Aftermath of the Midnight Bells

As the bells fell silent, the villagers stood in awe, the magic of the moment lingering in the air. They turned to see Clare descending from the tower, her face glowing with an inner light. She joined the crowd, feeling a new sense of belonging and warmth.

"What did the bells show you?" one of the elders asked gently.

Clare smiled, her eyes shining. "They showed me that the ones we love are always with us, no matter where they are. And that the magic of Christmas is found in the love we share."

The villagers nodded, understanding the wisdom in her words. That night, they returned to their homes with hearts lightened and spirits lifted. The tolling of the Midnight Bells had unlocked not just secrets, but the timeless truth that love is the greatest magic of all.

The Legacy of the Midnight Bells

From that Christmas Eve onward, the Midnight Bells of Hartshollow rang every year at midnight, a symbol of hope, love, and the magic of the season. Clare's story became a cherished part of the village lore, reminding people of the power of a selfless wish and the enduring presence of love.

The bells continue to chime each Christmas Eve, resonating through the village and beyond. It is said that if you listen closely as the bells toll, you might hear a whisper of the secrets they hold—a reminder that the spirit of Christmas lives in the hearts of those who dare to hope, love, and believe in the magic of the Midnight Bells.

Chapter 22: The Silent Night

There is a special kind of magic that descends upon the world on Christmas Eve, an almost ethereal hush that blankets everything in stillness. This phenomenon is known as *The Silent Night,* a time when the earth seems to pause, holding its breath in the anticipation of Christmas. Some say that on this night, the barriers between the worlds of reality and dreams grow thin, allowing a fleeting glimpse of something wondrous and eternal. This story unfolds within that quiet power, a tale of reflection, redemption, and the transformative magic that only a silent night can bring.

The Village of Hemlock Hollow

Nestled deep in a snow-covered valley, surrounded by dark pine forests and towering hills, lay the village of Hemlock Hollow. The villagers lived in harmony with the changing seasons, embracing the long, harsh winters as a time for warmth, community, and the festivities of Christmas. However, this year, an unspoken heaviness hung over the village.

Hemlock Hollow had suffered a difficult year. The harvest had been sparse, and a bitter cold had set in early. People were weary, their spirits dampened by the trials they had faced. The usual laughter and songs that filled the streets during the Christmas season were replaced with quiet murmurs and the sound of wind sweeping through the narrow lanes.

The villagers had nearly forgotten the magic of Christmas Eve—that is, all except for an old woman named Elinora. Elinora lived on the outskirts of the village in a small, humble cottage. She was a quiet presence, known to have a deep connection with nature and the mysteries of the forest. Though she rarely ventured into the village, it was said that she possessed a wisdom born from years of solitude and reflection.

On this particular Christmas Eve, Elinora sensed a profound stillness settling over the valley. She could feel it in the air, a silence that was more than just the absence of noise—it was a silence filled with possibility. "The Silent Night is coming," she whispered to herself, looking out from her window at the forest bathed in the pale light of the rising moon.

The Wanderer's Arrival

As the night fell, casting its veil of quiet over the village, a lone figure approached Hemlock Hollow. He was a traveler, cloaked in a thick, tattered coat and carrying a worn pack over his shoulder. His name was Elias, a man who had been wandering the world for many years, driven by the mistakes of his past and the sorrow that accompanied them.

Elias had once been a man of wealth and pride, living in a distant city where he had chased power and riches, neglecting the love and friendships that had surrounded him. In his pursuit of success, he had pushed away those who cared for him, only to find himself alone when fortune finally turned against him. For years, he had roamed the countryside, searching for meaning, for redemption, but finding none.

The Silent Night had drawn him to Hemlock Hollow, though he did not understand why. As he entered the village, he was struck by the profound stillness that enveloped it. There were no bustling sounds, no laughter, not even the faintest echo of carols. Instead, there was only a deep, penetrating quiet that seemed to resonate through his very being.

Elias wandered through the snow-covered streets, feeling the weight of his solitude more acutely than ever. The windows of the cottages glowed with warm candlelight, but the silence pressed in on him, reminding him of the emptiness within his own heart.

At the edge of the village, he saw a faint light coming from a small cottage. Drawn to it, he approached and gently knocked on the door. After a moment, the door creaked open, and Elinora stood before him, her eyes sharp and kind.

"You seem lost, traveler," she said, her voice as soft as the falling snow. "Come inside and warm yourself."

Elias hesitated, unused to such simple kindness, but nodded and stepped into the warmth of the cottage. Elinora guided him to a chair by the fire, where he sat gratefully, feeling the warmth seep into his bones.

The Stillness of Reflection

For a while, they sat in silence, the crackling of the fire the only sound that filled the room. Elinora studied Elias, sensing the turmoil that brewed within him. "This night is unlike any other," she began quietly. "Do you know of the Silent Night?"

Elias shook his head. "I have heard of Christmas Eve, but not of the Silent Night."

Elinora nodded. "The Silent Night is a time when the world becomes still, allowing us to hear what lies within our hearts. It is a night when the past, present, and future converge, revealing truths that we often overlook in the noise of our lives."

Elias lowered his gaze to the fire, his thoughts swirling. "Then it is a night meant to torment those like me," he said bitterly. "For my heart is filled with regret, with the memories of things I cannot change."

Elinora tilted her head thoughtfully. "Regret is a heavy burden, but it is also a sign that your heart still seeks light. The Silent Night can be a time of redemption, if you allow yourself to listen."

The words hung in the air, and for a moment, everything seemed to grow even quieter. Outside, the wind had stilled, and the world was wrapped in a profound calmness. Elias closed his eyes, feeling the silence settle into his soul. It was as if the entire world had paused, waiting for something to emerge from the depths of the quiet.

In that silence, memories surfaced. He saw the faces of those he had wronged, the friends he had pushed away, and the joy he had sacrificed for fleeting ambitions. The images played out like a silent film, stirring emotions that he had long buried. And then, amidst the sorrow, he saw something unexpected—the moments of kindness, of love, that had been offered to him even when he had felt unworthy of them.

A tear slid down his cheek as he opened his eyes. "I wish... I wish I could go back," he whispered. "I wish I could change things."

Elinora placed a hand on his shoulder, her touch gentle yet grounding. "The past cannot be changed, Elias. But the Silent Night offers you something more precious—the chance to let go and begin anew. The silence is not here to torment you; it is here to heal you, if you let it."

The Silent Night's Gift

As the minutes ticked by, Elias felt a strange sensation wash over him. It was as if the quietness of the night was seeping into his being, soothing the turmoil within him. The silence became a presence, not one of emptiness, but of something warm, comforting, and understanding.

He took a deep breath, feeling his heart lighten. "How do I let go?" he asked, his voice barely a whisper.

"By embracing the silence," Elinora replied. "By forgiving yourself, and by choosing to carry the lessons of the past into a future where you can be a force of kindness."

Elias closed his eyes once more, allowing the silence to envelop him. In that moment, he felt a profound release, as if a weight he had carried for years was being lifted. The regrets, the guilt, the sorrow—they remained as memories, but they no longer defined him. The silence had brought him peace, the peace of understanding and self-forgiveness.

When he opened his eyes, he felt different, lighter. The fire crackled softly, and outside, the world lay still and serene. Elinora smiled at him, her eyes reflecting the warmth of the moment.

"The Silent Night has shown you its power," she said. "Remember, it is in the quietest moments that we often find the most profound truths."

The Dawn of Christmas

As the first light of dawn touched the horizon, Elias stood to leave. "Thank you," he said, his voice steady and filled with newfound resolve. "For reminding me of what truly matters."

Elinora nodded, her gaze warm. "Go now, and carry the peace of the Silent Night with you. It will guide you, even in the noisiest of days."

Elias stepped out of the cottage, feeling the crisp air of Christmas morning fill his lungs. The village lay quiet, wrapped in a soft, golden light. He walked through the streets, his heart open and unburdened, seeing the world with new eyes. The villagers, who had awoken to the dawn, greeted him with kindness, sensing the change in him.

From that day forward, Elias chose a different path. He remained in Hemlock Hollow, becoming a part of the community, offering help and friendship wherever it was needed. The shadows of his past did not vanish, but they no longer weighed him down. The Silent Night had taught him that redemption was not about changing the past, but about how one chose to live in the present.

Each year, when Christmas Eve arrived, the village would gather and honor the Silent Night, remembering its quiet power. And though no words were spoken during that sacred hour, the silence would fill their hearts with warmth, reminding them of the peace, hope, and love that Christmas truly brings.

The Eternal Power of the Silent Night

The story of the Silent Night endures, a tale of stillness that transforms hearts and reveals truths hidden by the clamor of daily life. It teaches that silence is not the absence of sound, but a presence in itself—one that allows us to reflect, forgive, and find the courage to begin anew.

And so, on every Christmas Eve, when the world grows quiet and the stars shine brightly in the sky, remember the power of the Silent Night. It is a time to listen to the whispers of the heart, to embrace peace, and to find strength in the quiet moments that connect us to something far greater than ourselves.

Chapter 23: Northern Lights' Secrets

The Northern Lights, or *Aurora Borealis*, are one of nature's most breathtaking phenomena. As they dance across the sky in hues of green, pink, and violet, they transform the heavens into a canvas of ethereal beauty. For centuries, these lights have inspired awe, wonder, and countless tales. To many, they are more than a spectacle; they are a bridge between the earthly world and the mystical realm. In this chapter, we will explore the mystical tales of the Northern Lights, delving into their magical connection to Christmas and the secrets they are believed to hold.

The Lights of the North: Nature's Mystical Display

Science explains the Northern Lights as the result of solar particles colliding with the Earth's atmosphere, creating stunning displays of light. However, for the people living in the northernmost regions of the world—where the nights are long and the winter air is crisp—the lights have always carried a deeper significance. In these cultures, the Aurora is seen as a harbinger of change, a messenger of the cosmos, and a sign that the world is imbued with magic during the winter months, especially around Christmas.

Legends tell of the Northern Lights as the spirits of the ancestors, of celestial beings dancing, or as pathways to other realms. When the lights shine most brilliantly during Christmas, they are said to reveal hidden truths, open portals to magical worlds, and grant wishes to those with pure hearts.

The Spirit Dance: The Legend of the Aurora Spirits

In the northern forests of Finland, there is an ancient legend that tells of the *Aurora Spirits*, ethereal beings who dwell within the lights. According to this tale, the spirits emerge from the stars to dance in the sky, celebrating the arrival of winter and the Christmas season.

Long ago, in a village near the edge of the Arctic Circle, lived a girl named Maarika. She was a quiet, thoughtful child who spent most of her days wandering through the snow-covered woods, listening to the whispering winds and watching the night sky. She had grown up hearing stories about the Northern Lights and the spirits that danced within them. Her grandmother would often say, "The Aurora Spirits are guardians of winter's secrets. They appear when the world is silent, bringing magic and wonder to those who truly believe."

One particularly harsh winter, the villagers faced difficult times. The snow was deep, the food stores were low, and illness had spread among the people. Despite the hardships, Maarika clung to the hope that the lights would bring a sign of better days.

On Christmas Eve, the sky was clear and the stars sparkled with an intensity that filled the air with a sense of anticipation. Maarika bundled herself in warm furs and ventured into the forest, her heart filled with a silent wish for her village to find peace and joy once more.

As she walked, she noticed a faint glow on the horizon. The glow grew brighter, and soon the Northern Lights appeared, sweeping across the sky in waves of green, blue, and violet. Maarika stopped in awe, her breath misting in the cold air.

The lights began to swirl and twist, forming shapes that danced and shimmered. In that moment, she felt the presence of something greater than herself, a sense of ancient power and kindness. Then, she heard it—a soft, melodic laughter, like the chiming of ice crystals in the wind. She squinted, and amidst the lights, she saw them: the Aurora Spirits.

They were ethereal beings, their forms shifting and glimmering like the lights themselves. They moved gracefully, their dance painting the sky with colors that seemed to pulse with life. Maarika watched in wonder as one of the spirits descended towards her, its eyes glowing with warmth.

"You are one of pure heart," the spirit spoke, its voice like a whisper carried on the breeze. "Your wish for your village has been heard."

Maarika's eyes widened. "You know my wish?"

The spirit nodded. "We are the guardians of winter's magic. When the world is most still, we listen to the hearts that beat with hope and love. Tonight, the lights shine not just for the beauty of the sky, but to bring warmth to those who believe."

The spirit lifted its hand, and from the lights above, a gentle cascade of shimmering flakes descended, sparkling like diamonds in the moonlight. The flakes drifted towards the village, filling the air with a soft, glowing mist.

"Go now, child," the spirit said, its form beginning to fade back into the swirling lights. "Return to your people, and know that the magic of the Aurora will watch over you."

With her heart full of wonder, Maarika turned and hurried back to the village. As she approached, she saw the glow of the Northern Lights still reflecting off the snow, casting an enchanting light over the cottages. To her amazement, the once-silent village was now filled with a sense of warmth and renewal. The sick were recovering, and the villagers emerged from their homes, eyes wide with awe as they felt the magic in the air.

From that night forward, the villagers of Maarika's village believed that the Northern Lights were more than just a natural phenomenon—they were the spirits of winter, bringing joy and hope to the world when it was needed most. The lights became a symbol of the miracles that Christmas could bring, if only one believed in their magic.

The Lights as Pathways: The Tale of the Celestial Road

Among the Inuit people of Greenland and Canada, the Northern Lights are known as *Aqsarniit*, or the "Pathway of Souls." It is said that the lights create a bridge between the earthly world and the spirit realm, a road that guides the souls of the departed to their resting place in the stars.

One ancient tale tells of a hunter named Nukka, who set out on a quest to find the lights' secrets. Nukka was a wise and brave man, respected in his community, yet he carried a sorrow within him that no one could ease—the loss of his beloved daughter, Akiak. She had passed away during a harsh winter, and ever since, Nukka had been haunted by grief and the longing to know that her spirit was at peace.

One cold Christmas Eve, as the sky darkened and the stars began to appear, Nukka climbed the tallest hill outside his village, hoping to catch a glimpse of the Northern Lights. As he reached the summit, the sky suddenly erupted in color. Bands of green and purple stretched across the horizon, shimmering with an almost otherworldly light.

Nukka stood still, his eyes fixed on the lights. His heart pounded with a mixture of awe and sorrow. He had heard stories that the lights could reveal the path of the souls and allow one to see the spirits of those who had passed. With all his being, he silently called out to the lights, his thoughts filled with the memory of Akiak.

For a long moment, nothing happened. Then, to his amazement, the lights began to shift and form into a road of brilliant colors that stretched across the sky. Along this road, Nukka saw faint figures moving gracefully, their forms surrounded by a soft, glowing light. His breath caught in his throat as one of the figures paused and turned towards him.

It was Akiak.

She appeared as a vision of light, her face serene and filled with joy. Though her form was ethereal, Nukka felt her presence with an intensity that warmed his heart. She raised a hand in greeting, her eyes filled with love and peace.

"Father," her voice echoed in his mind, as clear as if she stood beside him. "The lights are our path. They guide us to a place of beauty and harmony, where we watch over those we love."

Tears welled in Nukka's eyes as he watched the road of lights carry his daughter and the other spirits forward, toward the stars. A sense of peace washed over him, the weight of his sorrow lifting. He knew now that Akiak was not gone; she was part of the vast, magical tapestry of the Northern Lights, forever watching over him and the world below.

As the lights continued to dance, Nukka descended the hill, his heart lighter than it had been in years. From that night, he became a storyteller, sharing the tale of the Northern Lights as the road of the spirits, bringing comfort and hope to those who feared the loss of their loved ones.

The Lights and Christmas Wishes

In some Scandinavian traditions, it is believed that the Northern Lights shine brightest on Christmas Eve because they are imbued with the wishes of those who gaze upon them. It is said that if you stand under the lights and whisper your wish with a heart full of hope, the Aurora will carry it to the heavens, where it will be heard by the stars and possibly granted.

One such tale tells of a young boy named Erik, who lived in a small village near the fjords of Norway. Erik was known for his big heart and the simple wish he carried each Christmas: that his family and village would be safe and happy.

One Christmas Eve, while the rest of the village gathered for the holiday feast, Erik slipped away to the edge of the fjord. The sky above was clear, and the stars twinkled like diamonds against the dark canvas of the night. As he stood there, a faint glow appeared on the horizon, growing brighter until the Northern Lights spread across the sky in a dazzling display of greens and blues.

Erik closed his eyes and whispered his wish to the lights, "Please keep my family safe and bring happiness to our village."

To his surprise, the lights seemed to respond. They pulsed softly, as if acknowledging his words. Then, a stream of light descended, encircling Erik in a warm, comforting embrace. For a moment, he felt a profound sense of peace, as though the lights were assuring him that his wish had been heard.

When Erik returned to the village, he found the air filled with a joyous energy. The villagers, who had been struggling through the harsh winter, were now filled with laughter and warmth, their spirits lifted as if by some unseen force. From that night, Erik knew that the Northern

Lights held more than just beauty; they carried the magic of Christmas and the power of hope.

The Secrets of the Northern Lights

The Northern Lights are more than a natural phenomenon; they are a canvas upon which countless cultures and traditions have painted stories of magic, hope, and wonder. Whether seen as the dance of spirits, the celestial road, or a conduit for wishes, the lights remind us that the world is filled with mysteries far beyond our understanding.

As Christmas approaches and the lights shimmer in the northern skies, those who gaze upon them are invited to partake in their magic. They are a reminder that beauty exists even in the darkest nights, that the universe listens to the whispers of the heart, and that the spirit of Christmas transcends the earthly realm, connecting us to the stars and the infinite wonders of the cosmos.

So, the next time you find yourself beneath the Northern Lights, take a moment to listen to their secrets. Let their light fill you with awe and remind you that in the quiet beauty of the Christmas season, there is a touch of the eternal and the divine, waiting to be discovered.

Chapter 24: The Sleeping Snowman

The story of *The Sleeping Snowman* is unlike any other, for it invites readers to shape the journey of a magical snowman. You, the reader, will guide the snowman through a series of enchanting paths, each choice leading to a new twist in the tale. As you read, you'll encounter crossroads where you must decide the outcome of the snowman's adventure. Choose wisely, for each decision carries its own magic and consequence!

The Beginning: The Snowman Awakens

It was Christmas Eve in the cozy village of Pine Hollow, where the snow blanketed the ground in a thick, powdery layer. The villagers had spent the day building snowmen of all shapes and sizes, decorating them with scarves, hats, and twigs for arms. Among them stood a particularly grand snowman, sculpted by the children with great care and adorned with a red woolen scarf, a top hat, and a carrot nose.

As the night fell and the stars began to twinkle in the sky, a hush settled over the village. All was still, save for the whisper of the wind. It was in this quiet hour that magic stirred within the snowman. The moonlight shone upon his snowy form, causing a faint glow to emanate from within. His eyes—two coal-black buttons—blinked open, revealing a spark of life.

The snowman lifted his twiggy arms and stretched, feeling the magic coursing through him. "I'm... awake!" he exclaimed in a deep, friendly voice that echoed through the snow-covered square. But something puzzled him. Why had he awoken on this night? What was his purpose?

As he pondered, he noticed three paths before him, each leading to a different part of the village. He realized that he needed to choose his adventure.

Reader's Choice 1: Where should the Snowman go first?

- **A.** Follow the path to the glowing forest, where mysterious lights flicker among the trees.
- **B.** Walk towards the sound of laughter coming from the village square.
- **C.** Head to the frozen pond, where the ice glimmers under the moonlight.

If You Chose A: The Glowing Forest

The snowman decided to follow the path to the glowing forest. As he walked, the trees grew taller and denser, their branches heavy with snow. A soft, ethereal light glowed between the trunks, casting a magical ambiance over the forest floor.

As he ventured deeper, the snowman spotted tiny, twinkling lights flitting through the air. They were frost sprites, delicate creatures with wings like frost-covered leaves. They darted around the snowman, giggling softly.

"Welcome, snowman!" one of the sprites chirped. "You have awoken because of a wish made in this forest. We need your help to fulfill it!"

The snowman tilted his head, intrigued. "A wish, you say? What must I do?"

The sprites circled around him and pointed to a nearby clearing, where a small fir tree stood. Its branches were bare, save for a single ornament at its top—a glowing star.

"The tree is magical," the sprites explained. "But it has fallen asleep and needs to be woken up to fulfill the wish. You must decide how to wake it."

Option B: Walk towards the sound of laughter coming from the village square.

As you follow the sound of joyful laughter, the cold air is filled with the warmth of festive cheer. The snow crunches beneath your feet, and as you approach the village square, you're greeted by the sight of twinkling lights strung between quaint cottages, each window aglow with the golden light of candles.

In the center of the square stands a towering Christmas tree, its branches adorned with ornaments that glisten in the light of flickering lanterns. Beneath the tree, children run and play, their laughter ringing through the crisp winter air, while villagers huddle together, sharing stories and cups of hot cider. The smell of freshly baked gingerbread fills the square, and a small group of carolers begins to sing a familiar tune.

Choosing this path leads you into the heart of the village's Christmas festivities, where you are welcomed by the warmth of community and the magic of shared traditions. The joy here is infectious, and you find yourself swept up in the celebration, your worries melting away in the glow of the holiday spirit.

Option C: Head to the frozen pond, where the ice glimmers under the moonlight.

You decide to head towards the frozen pond, drawn by the ethereal glow of moonlight reflecting off the smooth surface of the ice. As you walk through the snow-dusted trees, the sounds of the village begin to fade, replaced by the quiet stillness of the forest. The night sky above is clear, stars twinkling like tiny gems against a canvas of deep blue, while the full moon bathes the world in a soft, silvery light.

The pond comes into view, its frozen surface glistening like glass beneath the moonlight. A light mist hovers over the ice, creating an almost otherworldly atmosphere. The air is crisp, and a peaceful silence surrounds you. Nearby, you spot an old wooden bench and decide to sit for a moment, taking in the tranquil beauty of the scene.

This path offers a quiet, reflective moment, away from the festivities of the village. Here, in the stillness of the night, you feel a sense of calm and wonder, as if the world itself is pausing to appreciate the magic of the season. It's a place for peaceful contemplation, where the beauty of winter's landscape feels almost enchanted.

Reader's Choice 2: How will the Snowman wake the tree?

- **A.** Sing a song to the tree, filling the air with the melody of Christmas.
- **B.** Touch the tree with his twig arm, sharing the magic within him.
- **C.** Find the star at the top of the tree and whisper the wish into it.

If You Chose A: Sing a Song to the Tree

The snowman took a deep breath (as much as a snowman could) and began to sing. His voice was rich and deep, carrying the timeless melody of a Christmas carol. As the notes filled the forest, the tree began to tremble. Its branches shook, and tiny green shoots sprouted, unfurling like new life.

With each verse, the tree came more alive. The lights on its branches flickered on, casting a warm glow across the clearing. The star at the top gleamed brightly, sending a beam of light skyward.

"The wish has been fulfilled!" the sprites cheered, their wings fluttering with excitement. "You have woken the tree, and now the wish will spread across the forest, bringing joy and magic to all who dwell here."

The snowman beamed with pride, feeling the warmth of Christmas magic flow through him. His journey in the forest was complete, but more adventures awaited as he turned back to the village...

(From here, you can guide the snowman back to explore other paths, continuing his adventure.)

If You Chose B: Touch the Tree with His Twig Arm

The snowman approached the tree and gently touched its trunk with his twig arm. As he did, a spark of magic passed from him into the tree. A soft hum resonated through the air as the tree's branches began to glow with a frosty light. The snow covering its needles melted away, revealing vibrant green foliage.

The star atop the tree brightened, casting light throughout the forest. Snowflakes began to fall gently, sparkling as they touched the ground. The wish had been fulfilled, bringing life and light to the forest on this magical night.

"Well done, snowman!" the sprites sang joyously. "You have awakened the tree and the magic within it. The forest shall now be a place of wonder for all who visit."

With the task completed, the snowman nodded to the sprites and made his way back to the village, his adventure far from over...

If You Chose C: Whisper the Wish into the Star

With determination, the snowman approached the tree and carefully climbed its branches. As he reached the top, he gazed at the glowing star and whispered, "Let the magic of Christmas bring warmth and joy to all."

The star pulsed with light, growing brighter and brighter until it bathed the entire forest in a golden glow. The tree's branches rustled, and new ornaments appeared, hanging like glistening jewels. The wish spread through the air, bringing a feeling of peace and joy to every corner of the forest.

"You've done it!" the sprites cheered. "The wish has awakened the magic of the forest!"

The snowman climbed down, his heart filled with a sense of fulfillment. His adventure continued as he made his way back to the village...

Reader's Choice 3: How should the Snowman help light the lanterns?

- **A.** Use a magical snowflake to ignite the lanterns.
- **B.** Share a story of hope to inspire the villagers to light them.
- **C.** Lead the children in a circle around the tree, using their laughter to spark the light.

Option A: Use a magical snowflake to ignite the lanterns.

The Snowman gently raises his mittened hand and, with a flick of his wrist, summons a magical snowflake that twirls gracefully in the air. The flake shimmers with a brilliant light, glowing with hues of silver and blue as it floats delicately down to the first lantern. As soon as it touches the wick, a small flame springs to life, casting a warm, golden glow across the snow-covered square.

One by one, the snowflake flutters from lantern to lantern, igniting each one with a soft crackle. The light spreads across the village, illuminating the square with a magical radiance. The villagers watch in awe, their faces lit with wonder, as the Snowman's enchanted snowflake brings warmth and light to their holiday celebration. The scene feels like a fairy tale, filled with the mystery and magic of the season.

Choosing this option reveals the Snowman's mystical powers and highlights the magic that runs through this enchanted village, where even the simplest act—like lighting lanterns—becomes an unforgettable moment of wonder.

Option B: Share a story of hope to inspire the villagers to light them.

Instead of using magic, the Snowman gathers the villagers around the tree, his presence calming the crowd. With a twinkle in his eyes, he begins to tell a story—a tale of hope that transcends time. The story speaks of a village not unlike their own, long ago, where a single lantern, lit in the darkest hour, brought warmth and unity to the hearts of everyone who saw it. It was not just the light, but the hope it symbolized, that spread joy and inspired the villagers to carry the light forward.

Moved by the Snowman's words, the villagers each take a lantern in their hands, lighting them one by one. The flicker of each flame represents their own belief in the power of hope, kindness, and togetherness. The square soon glows with the warm light of countless lanterns, but it is the shared sense of purpose and community that truly illuminates the night.

By choosing this option, the Snowman's ability to inspire through storytelling is emphasized, showing that the true magic of Christmas lies not just in actions, but in the spirit of hope and connection that binds people together.

Option C: Lead the children in a circle around the tree, using their laughter to spark the light.

With a joyful smile, the Snowman gently beckons the children to join him by the tree. Their faces light up as they gather around, their breath visible in the chilly night air. "Let's make some magic together!" the Snowman declares, clapping his snowy hands. The children giggle, their laughter bubbling up like the sound of jingling bells.

Hand in hand, the Snowman and the children begin to circle the tree, their laughter growing louder with each step. As they move faster, a sparkling energy fills the air, swirling above them in a golden arc. Their joyful sounds rise like a song, and suddenly, with a burst of brilliance, the lanterns around the square flicker to life, ignited by the pure, radiant power of their laughter.

The village square is soon aglow, not just with the light of the lanterns, but with the happiness that only the laughter of children can bring. The villagers cheer, and the Snowman beams, knowing that the true magic of the night was in the joy they created together.

Choosing this option highlights the playful and joyful spirit of the Snowman and the children, showing that sometimes the most powerful magic comes from shared happiness and the simple delight of laughter.

Reader's Choice 4: What gift does the Snowman choose?

- **A.** The Gift of Laughter, to bring joy to the village.
- **B.** The Gift of Warmth, to melt sorrow and fear.
- **C.** The Gift of Light, to illuminate paths in darkness.

Option A: The Gift of Laughter, to bring joy to the village.

The Snowman, with his signature twinkle in his eyes, knows exactly what the village needs most. He reaches into his snowy chest and pulls out a sparkling bell, infused with the *Gift of Laughter*. The moment he holds it high, the bell jingles with a melody so infectious that it sends waves of joy through the air. The villagers can't help but smile as they hear it. Children begin to giggle uncontrollably, and even the sternest faces soften into laughter.

The sound spreads like magic, filling every corner of the village square, and soon the entire town is enveloped in a chorus of joyous laughter. The once cold winter night is now warmed by the sound of pure, unfiltered joy. The villagers' worries and fears melt away as they share in the merriment, reminded that even in the darkest moments, laughter has the power to bring lightness and connection.

Choosing this gift brings a sense of lightheartedness to the story, emphasizing the importance of joy and laughter as a way to unite and uplift the village. It shows that sometimes, a simple laugh is the greatest gift of all.

Option B: The Gift of Warmth, to melt sorrow and fear.

With a knowing nod, the Snowman selects the *Gift of Warmth*, understanding that the village needs more than physical heat—it needs the warmth that comes from love, compassion, and community. He extends his snowy arms and conjures a glowing ember, small but powerful. As he presents the gift, the ember bursts into a gentle, radiant glow that immediately spreads warmth throughout the village.

The villagers feel it first in their hearts, as a deep, soothing sensation that chases away the coldness of sorrow and fear. It spreads to their hands and feet, warming them both inside and out. The warmth fosters a sense of togetherness, melting away feelings of loneliness, grief, and doubt. Families embrace, neighbors exchange kind words, and the entire village seems to come alive with the comfort of shared affection.

This gift emphasizes the Snowman's wisdom and compassion, showing that true warmth doesn't come from a fire, but from the love and care people show one another. It highlights the power of emotional warmth in fostering a sense of belonging and unity.

Option C: The Gift of Light, to illuminate paths in darkness.

The Snowman, sensing that the village is in need of guidance and hope, chooses the *Gift of Light*. With a gentle motion, he reaches up to the night sky and plucks a single, shining star from the heavens. The star glows brighter in his hands, its light pure and steady. He places it gently in the center of the village square, where it shines brilliantly, casting away the shadows.

The villagers are in awe as the light grows, illuminating not just the square, but every dark corner of the village. Paths that were once hidden in shadow are now clear, both physically and metaphorically. The light represents guidance, hope, and clarity—showing the way forward in times of uncertainty. Under the star's glow, the villagers feel their burdens lift, and new possibilities open before them.

By choosing the Gift of Light, the Snowman brings a deeper sense of purpose to the story, symbolizing how even in the darkest moments, a single light can lead the way. It's a gift of hope and renewal, offering the village a chance to move forward with courage and optimism.

The Snowman's Adventure Continues

Each choice you make for the snowman shapes his journey, revealing new aspects of the world around him and the magic of Christmas. Whether he awakens the forest, helps the villagers, or discovers secrets beneath the ice, the snowman embodies the spirit of joy, kindness, and the wonder of the season.

And so, dear reader, the adventure of the *Sleeping Snowman* rests in your hands. Follow his paths, make his choices, and uncover the magic that lies within this enchanting tale. For each decision creates a new story, and every story holds the essence of Christmas's quiet, wondrous power.

Chapter 25: Yuletide Beasts

The magic of Christmas is often associated with joy, warmth, and goodwill, but hidden within the winter tales are stories of darker creatures that emerge during the season. These *Yuletide Beasts* serve as cautionary figures, embodying the consequences of greed, misbehavior, and neglect. They come from the old myths and traditions of different cultures, bringing a sense of mystery and shadow to the otherwise light-filled festivities. This chapter delves into these eerie tales, exploring the legends of Krampus, the Yule Cat, and other mythical creatures that lurk in the shadows of Christmas lore.

The Shadow of St. Nicholas: The Tale of Krampus

Among the most infamous of the Yuletide Beasts is *Krampus*, a horned, demonic figure who emerges from the depths of Alpine folklore. Krampus is known as the shadow of St. Nicholas, representing the darker side of Christmas. While St. Nicholas rewards good children with gifts and sweets, Krampus punishes those who have been naughty, serving as a stark reminder of the consequences of bad behavior.

1. The Origins of Krampus

The legend of Krampus dates back to pre-Christian Alpine traditions, where he was believed to be a pagan spirit of the forest. His name is derived from the German word *krampen*, meaning "claw." With the spread of Christianity, Krampus was integrated into Christmas customs as a counterbalance to the generous and benevolent St. Nicholas.

Described as a creature with the horns of a goat, the fur of a beast, and the face of a demon, Krampus carries chains, which he rattles to announce his presence. He often has a bundle of birch sticks, used to whip those who have misbehaved, and a sack or basket on his back to carry away especially naughty children.

2. The Night of Krampus: December 5th

In the Alpine regions of Austria, Germany, and other parts of Europe, December 5th is known as *Krampusnacht*, or Krampus Night. On this night, it is said that Krampus roams the streets, seeking out children who have been unruly throughout the year. Dressed in fur, horns, and a fearsome mask, Krampus is accompanied by the jingling of bells and the clanking of chains.

Families prepare for Krampusnacht by leaving offerings of fruit, nuts, and sweets outside their doors in the hopes of appeasing the beast and avoiding his wrath. Children, too, are reminded of Krampus's looming presence as a warning to behave during the long winter months.

Legend has it that if Krampus finds a particularly naughty child, he might punish them with a swat from his birch sticks or even carry them away in his sack to his lair deep in the mountains. However, Krampus's purpose is not simply to frighten; he serves as a reminder that the spirit of Christmas is not just about gifts and merriment but also about kindness, respect, and good behavior.

The Yule Cat: Iceland's Fearsome Feline

In the land of fire and ice—Iceland—there exists a tale of a creature that roams the snowy countryside during Christmas. The *Jólakötturinn*, or the *Yule Cat*, is no ordinary feline. It is a monstrous beast, large enough to tower over houses, with eyes that glow like embers in the winter darkness. The Yule Cat is known to lurk in the shadows, waiting for an opportunity to pounce on the careless and the lazy.

1. The Yule Cat and the Tradition of New Clothes

The legend of the Yule Cat is tied to an old Icelandic tradition surrounding the Christmas season. According to the tale, those who did not receive new clothes for Christmas would be at risk of being devoured by the Yule Cat. This tradition stems from the practice of wool production in Iceland. Farmers would reward workers with new clothes if they completed their work on time, thereby ensuring that everyone was industrious during the short winter days.

The Yule Cat prowls the snow-covered hills and villages, peering into windows to see who has been given new clothes. If a person has worked hard and received their new garments, they are safe from the Yule Cat's wrath. However, those who have neglected their duties or failed to receive new clothing must beware, for the Yule Cat is said to snatch them up in the night.

While the Yule Cat may seem like a terrifying beast, its story serves as a reminder of the importance of diligence, generosity, and the spirit of giving. By ensuring that everyone has something new to wear for Christmas, the Yule Cat myth encourages a sense of community and care during the cold, dark months of winter.

2. The Yule Cat's Connection to Gryla and the Yule Lads

The Yule Cat is not the only creature of Icelandic Christmas folklore. It is said to be the pet of *Gryla*, a fearsome troll who lives in the mountains, and the mother of the mischievous *Yule Lads*. Gryla is known for her insatiable appetite for naughty children, whom she boils in her cauldron. The Yule Lads, on the other hand, are a group of thirteen troll-like figures who come down from the mountains one by one during the days leading up to Christmas, each with their own unique and often troublesome behavior.

Together, Gryla, the Yule Lads, and the Yule Cat form a trio of dark Christmas figures, reminding children that good behavior is paramount during the festive season. While the Yule Lads have evolved into more playful and humorous characters in modern times, the Yule Cat remains a symbol of the consequences of idleness and selfishness.

The Kallikantzaroi: Greece's Christmas Goblins

In Greece and other parts of southeastern Europe, the Christmas season is haunted by mischievous goblins known as the *Kallikantzaroi*. These creatures are believed to dwell underground for most of the year, where they spend their time sawing away at the World Tree, which holds up the earth. During the Twelve Days of Christmas, however, the Kallikantzaroi are said to emerge to wreak havoc on the world above.

1. The Mischief of the Kallikantzaroi

The Kallikantzaroi are depicted as small, dark-skinned creatures with sharp teeth, hairy bodies, and a propensity for causing trouble. They are not necessarily malevolent, but they delight in creating chaos wherever they go. During their time on the surface, they are known to enter homes through chimneys, steal food, hide belongings, and play pranks on unsuspecting villagers.

To ward off the Kallikantzaroi, families would burn a Yule log continuously for the twelve days of Christmas, believing that the light and warmth would keep the goblins at bay. Additionally, hanging garlic or placing a colander outside the door were thought to confuse the goblins, as they would become obsessed with counting the holes in the colander, forgetting to enter the house.

2. The Return to the Underworld

As Epiphany approaches on January 6th, the Kallikantzaroi are driven back underground, where they resume their work of sawing at the World Tree. However, legend states that during their time above ground, the tree has healed itself, thus ensuring that the goblins must start their efforts all over again. This cycle serves as a reminder of the balance between light and darkness, order and chaos, that exists within the world.

The Kallikantzaroi's mischief is not meant to harm but rather to remind people of the need for vigilance and the importance of maintaining a sense of humor during the festive season. They embody the unpredictable and wild nature of winter, adding an element of playful danger to the Christmas festivities.

The Belsnickel: The Ragged Christmas Visitor

Originating in the folklore of southwestern Germany and brought to America by the Pennsylvania Dutch, *Belsnickel* is a figure who embodies both the kindness and severity of Christmas. Dressed in ragged clothes, fur, and sometimes a mask, Belsnickel appears during the weeks leading up to Christmas, carrying a sack of treats in one hand and a switch in the other.

1. The Dual Nature of Belsnickel

Belsnickel is both a gift-bringer and a disciplinarian. Unlike St. Nicholas, who arrives in splendor, Belsnickel is rugged and imposing, his presence often stirring both excitement and fear in children. He enters homes unannounced, and his first question is always directed at the children: "Have you been good?"

If the children have behaved, Belsnickel rewards them with candies, nuts, and fruits from his sack. However, if they have been naughty, they may receive a light tap from his switch as a warning to mend their ways. Belsnickel's visit serves as a reminder that Christmas is not merely about receiving gifts, but about reflecting on one's actions and striving to be good and kind.

2. A Lesson in Humility

The legend of Belsnickel is rooted in the tradition of humble introspection. His ragged appearance and stern demeanor contrast sharply with the opulence often associated with Christmas, teaching that the true spirit of the season lies not in material wealth, but in the sincerity of one's heart and actions. Belsnickel's role as both punisher and giver of gifts makes him a unique figure among the Yuletide Beasts, one who walks the line between fear and kindness.

The Dark and Light of Christmas Lore

The tales of these Yuletide Beasts may seem dark and foreboding, but they carry deeper messages that resonate with the spirit of Christmas. Krampus, the Yule Cat, the Kallikantzaroi, and Belsnickel each serve as reminders of the balance between good and bad, reward and consequence, light and shadow. They emphasize the importance of kindness, hard work, community, and the joy that comes from embracing the spirit of the season with an open heart.

While these creatures may not visit every Christmas, their stories linger, adding a touch of mystery and caution to the festivities. They remind us that Christmas, while filled with joy and light, also has room for reflection on our actions and the values we uphold.

As you sit by the warmth of the fire this Christmas, sharing stories and laughter, spare a thought for the Yuletide Beasts that roam the winter nights. They are part of the grand tapestry of Christmas lore, embodying both the wonder and the shadows that make the season so rich and profound.

Part 6: *Celebrating the Heart: Family, Friends, and Festivities*

Chapter 26: Christmas Eve Traditions

Christmas Eve is a night filled with magic, anticipation, and togetherness. It's a time when families gather, creating cherished memories through traditions both old and new. These traditions, from storytelling by the fire to preparing a midnight feast, transform the evening into a celebration that connects the past, present, and future. This chapter provides a detailed exploration of Christmas Eve traditions, framed through the cozy narrative of one family's warm and festive celebration.

The Hartley Family Christmas Eve

In the Hartley household, Christmas Eve had always been the most anticipated night of the year. Their traditions were a blend of customs passed down through generations, and each activity added a layer of joy and meaning to their celebration. The story of their Christmas Eve captures the magic of the season, offering ideas and inspiration for families looking to enrich their own festivities.

1. Decorating the Christmas Tree

As the sun began to set, casting a golden glow over the snow-covered landscape, the Hartley family gathered around their Christmas tree, ready to add the final touches. The tree, a tall and fragrant pine, stood proudly in the corner of the living room, its branches already adorned with twinkling lights and shimmering garlands.

"Time for the ornaments!" Mrs. Hartley announced, opening a box filled with a collection of treasures accumulated over the years. Each ornament told a story: the porcelain angel from Great-Grandmother's time, the homemade felt stars crafted by the children, and the glittering glass balls bought during family vacations.

The children, Sarah and Luke, eagerly selected their favorite ornaments. "I want to hang the snowman!" Luke exclaimed, holding up a chubby, smiling snowman with a red scarf.

Sarah chose the delicate, hand-painted reindeer. "This one goes near the top," she declared, carefully reaching up to place it on a branch.

Mr. Hartley brought over the final ornament—the star for the top of the tree. With everyone's hands steadying the ladder, Sarah climbed up to set the star in place. As it caught the glow of the lights, the tree sparkled, casting a warm, magical light across the room.

Tradition Tip: Decorating the tree on Christmas Eve can be a special ritual that brings the family together. Consider adding a new ornament each year, one that represents a memorable moment or milestone, to make the tree a living archive of shared experiences.

2. Preparing the Christmas Eve Feast

With the tree now complete, the delicious aromas of Christmas Eve dinner filled the house. The kitchen was the heart of the home during the holiday season, and Mrs. Hartley, wearing her festive apron, stirred pots on the stove and checked dishes in the oven.

"Who's ready to help make the gingerbread cookies?" she called out, her voice filled with excitement. The children raced into the kitchen, eager to join in the baking. They rolled out the dough, cut out shapes with cookie cutters—gingerbread men, stars, and Christmas trees—and decorated them with icing and candies.

While the cookies baked, Mr. Hartley prepared a pot of mulled cider, filling the air with the scent of cinnamon, cloves, and oranges. Mrs. Hartley, meanwhile, arranged a platter of cheeses, fruits, and nuts for the family to enjoy as appetizers.

Finally, the table was set with care: the centerpiece was a simple arrangement of pine branches and candles, surrounded by a spread of roasted meats, vegetables, warm bread, and the freshly baked cookies. The family sat down, holding hands as Mr. Hartley said a few words of gratitude for the food, the warmth of their home, and the joy of being together.

Tradition Tip: Preparing a special meal on Christmas Eve can be a meaningful tradition. Involve everyone in the kitchen, assigning tasks such as baking cookies, preparing appetizers, or setting the table. Sharing the labor of love creates a deeper sense of connection and accomplishment.

3. A Toast to the Season

After dinner, the family gathered in the living room for a Christmas toast. Mr. Hartley poured hot chocolate into mugs for the children and mulled wine for the adults, filling the room with the rich scent of spices.

"To love, laughter, and a season of joy," Mrs. Hartley said, raising her mug with a smile. "May this Christmas be as warm and wonderful as every year before."

"To Christmas!" the children chimed in, clinking their mugs together. The warmth of the drinks and the glow of the fire created a moment of pure contentment.

Tradition Tip: A Christmas Eve toast is a simple yet heartfelt tradition. Choose a beverage that everyone can enjoy, such as hot chocolate, mulled cider, or a festive punch, and take turns expressing a holiday wish or something for which each person is grateful.

4. Sharing Christmas Stories

With the warmth of the fire crackling and everyone cozied up in their favorite chairs, it was time for the next tradition: storytelling. Mrs. Hartley reached for a leather-bound book on the mantel, its cover embossed with gold letters reading, *"Christmas Tales for Young and Old."*

"Tonight, let's read 'The Nutcracker,'" she suggested, and the children nodded eagerly.

As she began to read, her voice filled the room with the magic of the story. The tale of Clara, the Nutcracker, and the Mouse King unfolded, transporting everyone to a world of dancing snowflakes and sugar plum fairies. The children listened intently, their eyes wide with wonder as they imagined the story coming to life.

When the story ended, Mr. Hartley took over. "Now, it's time for our own Christmas memories," he said, smiling. Each family member took turns sharing a favorite Christmas memory from years past—the year they built the giant snow fort, the time they sang carols through the village, and the year they adopted their cat, Mittens, on Christmas Eve.

Tradition Tip: Reading stories and sharing personal Christmas memories is a wonderful way to connect with the past and keep traditions alive. Choose a classic Christmas story to read aloud, then invite everyone to share their favorite holiday memories, creating a tapestry of family history.

5. The Christmas Eve Gift Exchange

Next came the tradition of the *Christmas Eve gift*. The Hartleys had a special rule: on Christmas Eve, each person could open one gift, but it had to be something small, often something that could be enjoyed immediately, like cozy socks, a new book, or a sweet treat.

The children eagerly reached for their gifts under the tree. Sarah unwrapped a beautifully illustrated book of Christmas crafts, while Luke opened a set of colorful mittens that matched his winter coat.

For Mr. Hartley, Mrs. Hartley had wrapped a jar of his favorite homemade spiced jam, and he smiled warmly as he untied the ribbon. For Mrs. Hartley, Mr. Hartley had chosen a soft, knitted scarf in her favorite shade of blue.

The room was filled with laughter and smiles as they admired their small but thoughtful gifts, each one chosen with love.

Tradition Tip: A Christmas Eve gift exchange can be a meaningful ritual, setting the tone for the night. Consider choosing gifts that encourage togetherness, such as a family board game, matching pajamas, or ingredients for a special treat to enjoy during the evening.

6. Lighting the Candle of Hope

As midnight approached, the final tradition began. Mrs. Hartley brought out a single white candle, placing it on the windowsill. This was the *Candle of Hope*, a family tradition that had been passed down for generations.

"Let us light this candle to symbolize hope, peace, and love," she said softly, striking a match. The flame flickered to life, casting a gentle glow that filled the room with warmth.

Each family member took a moment to silently make a wish for the coming year. The room grew quiet, filled with the magic of hope and the promise that Christmas brings.

Tradition Tip: Lighting a candle on Christmas Eve can be a powerful tradition. It symbolizes the light of hope, love, and peace. Allow each family member to make a wish or share a silent prayer, creating a moment of reflection amidst the excitement.

7. Bedtime and the Christmas Eve Surprise

Finally, it was time to prepare for bed. The children slipped into their new pajamas and placed a plate of cookies and a glass of milk on the hearth for Santa. As they climbed into bed, Mrs. Hartley tucked them in, whispering, "Sleep well, my darlings. Tomorrow is Christmas."

The children closed their eyes, dreaming of reindeer, snow, and the wonders of Christmas Day. Meanwhile, the parents crept back to the living room to add the final touches: filling stockings with little surprises and placing a few more gifts under the tree.

Tradition Tip: Establishing a bedtime ritual, such as leaving out treats for Santa or hanging stockings, adds to the magic of Christmas Eve. It also provides a quiet moment to savor the anticipation and joy of Christmas morning.

A Night of Love and Magic

As the house grew silent and the candle flickered in the window, the Hartleys settled into their beds, their hearts full and warm. Christmas Eve had woven its magic through each tradition, connecting the family in a tapestry of love, joy, and cherished memories.

This night, filled with light, laughter, and togetherness, became the foundation upon which the spirit of Christmas was built in their home. Each tradition, whether old or newly created, added to the enchantment of the season, reminding them that the greatest gift was the time spent together.

Tradition Tip: The beauty of Christmas Eve lies in the traditions that make it special for your family. Whether it's decorating the tree, sharing stories, exchanging a small gift, or simply lighting a candle, these rituals create moments of connection that become cherished memories for years to come.

As the clock struck midnight, the Hartleys drifted into a peaceful sleep, dreaming of the joy and wonder that awaited them with the dawn of Christmas Day. And so, the warmth of their Christmas Eve traditions wrapped around them like a cozy blanket, filling their home with the true spirit of the season.

Chapter 27: The Perfect Stocking

The tradition of hanging stockings on Christmas Eve is one of the most delightful aspects of the holiday season. For generations, children and adults alike have looked forward to the excitement of waking up on Christmas morning to find their stockings brimming with small gifts, treats, and trinkets. Stockings capture the joy of surprise and the spirit of giving in a way that resonates with all ages. This chapter delves into the origins of this beloved custom, shares heartwarming stocking stories, and offers creative activities for crafting and filling the *perfect stocking*.

The Origins of the Christmas Stocking Tradition

The tradition of hanging stockings can be traced back to old European legends, the most popular of which involves the kindly figure of St. Nicholas. According to the story, St. Nicholas, known for his generosity, heard of a poor widower with three daughters who had no money for their dowries. One night, as the family slept, St. Nicholas secretly slipped into their home and placed gold coins in the stockings the daughters had hung by the fireplace to dry. When the girls awoke the next morning, they discovered the coins and were overjoyed. From this act of kindness, the tradition of filling stockings with gifts was born.

Today, stockings are a symbol of Christmas cheer, often hung by the fireplace or at the foot of the bed. They are filled with small surprises, both practical and whimsical, making them a cherished part of Christmas celebrations.

The Hartley Family's Stocking Tradition

The Hartley family, introduced in the previous chapter, had a tradition of creating *the perfect stocking* for each family member, taking great care to personalize the contents. Each year, they added new elements to their stockings, building on the joy and creativity of the tradition. Their story offers a warm, illustrative look at how stockings can become a highlight of the holiday.

1. Choosing the Stockings

It was a chilly evening in early December when the Hartleys began their stocking preparations. The stockings, kept in a special box throughout the year, were brought out and dusted off. Each stocking was unique: Sarah's was adorned with glittery snowflakes, while Luke's featured a red-nosed reindeer. Mr. Hartley's stocking was a classic red with a green trim, and Mrs. Hartley's had an embroidered wreath with tiny bells.

Before filling the stockings, the family gathered around the kitchen table to discuss new ideas for the year's stocking stuffers. They cherished the tradition of choosing thoughtful items that reflected the recipient's personality, hobbies, and current interests.

Activity Tip: Allow each family member to choose or personalize their stocking. Whether it's through embroidery, fabric paint, or added embellishments, personalizing stockings makes them special and unique. For families crafting new stockings, consider a DIY session to decorate plain ones with fabric markers, sequins, or patches.

2. Crafting Homemade Stocking Stuffers

Part of the Hartley family's tradition involved crafting homemade gifts to place in the stockings. They dedicated an evening to making small items, filling the house with creativity and laughter.

- **For Sarah:** Luke decided to make a *friendship bracelet* using colorful embroidery threads. He carefully braided the threads, adding beads that spelled out Sarah's name. "She'll love this," he said proudly, holding up the bracelet to admire his work.
- **For Luke:** Sarah crafted a set of *decorated bookmarks*, knowing how much Luke loved to read. She cut small strips of cardstock, decorated them with holiday-themed stickers, and tied a ribbon at the top of each. "This way, he'll never lose his place in his favorite books," she explained with a smile.
- **For Mr. and Mrs. Hartley:** The children worked together to create a small jar of *hot chocolate mix*. They layered cocoa powder, sugar, mini marshmallows, and chocolate chips in a clear jar, sealing it with a red ribbon. On the tag, they wrote: *"To keep you warm and cozy on a snowy Christmas morning."*

Activity Tip: Homemade stocking stuffers add a personal touch. Consider crafting simple gifts like friendship bracelets, decorated bookmarks, or hot chocolate mixes. These thoughtful items not only fill the stockings but also carry the love and effort put into making them.

3. The Art of the Stocking Stuffer Hunt

Another part of the Hartleys' tradition was the *Stocking Stuffer Hunt*. A few days before Christmas, the family would visit local shops and markets, searching for small treasures to fill each other's stockings.

"Remember, it's the little things that matter," Mrs. Hartley would say as they strolled through the market, eyeing stalls filled with hand-made trinkets, candies, and quirky gadgets. The hunt was about finding items that brought joy, humor, or comfort—things that might be overlooked in the rush for larger presents but carried a world of delight in their simplicity.

- **For Mr. Hartley:** Sarah found a small tin of gourmet coffee beans. "Dad loves his morning coffee," she said. "He'll appreciate this."
- **For Mrs. Hartley:** Luke chose a set of tiny scented candles, each one with a different winter fragrance. "Mom loves lighting candles in the evening," he reasoned.

Activity Tip: Make the process of finding stocking stuffers an event in itself. Visit holiday markets or local shops with the goal of finding small, meaningful gifts. This activity not only fosters family togetherness but also adds an element of adventure to the tradition.

4. The Stocking Stuffer Checklist

Back at home, the Hartleys gathered around the table to review their *Stocking Stuffer Checklist*, ensuring that each stocking contained a mix of items. Their checklist included:

- **A Sweet Treat:** Chocolate coins, candy canes, or a small bag of homemade fudge.
- **Something Practical:** Cozy socks, lip balm, or a mini hand cream.
- **A Personal Item:** A keychain, a small book, or a custom-made trinket.
- **A Fun Surprise:** A small toy, a puzzle, or a novelty gadget.
- **A Sentimental Keepsake:** A handwritten note, a photo keychain, or a handmade craft.

Satisfied with their choices, they placed each item in the appropriate stocking, taking care to arrange them so that the most exciting gifts peeked out from the top. The stockings were then hung by the fireplace, ready for the magic of Christmas morning.

Activity Tip: Create your own Stocking Stuffer Checklist to ensure a well-rounded and thoughtful assortment of items. Include a variety of categories to balance fun, practicality, and sentimentality. This checklist can be adapted year after year to suit the family's evolving interests.

5. The Mystery Gift

Every year, the Hartleys included a *mystery gift* in each stocking—an item wrapped in colorful paper and placed at the very bottom. The identity of the giver remained a secret until Christmas morning, adding an element of surprise and guessing fun to the tradition.

On Christmas morning, Sarah pulled out the mystery gift from her stocking. It was a small, beautifully wrapped box. "Who put this in here?" she asked, eyes wide with excitement. The family exchanged glances and shrugged, feigning innocence.

When she opened it, she found a delicate silver locket with a picture of her and Luke inside. "I love it!" she exclaimed, hugging her brother. "Thank you, Luke!"

Luke grinned, his face lighting up. "I thought you might like something to keep us close, even when we're apart," he said.

Activity Tip: Incorporate a mystery gift into each stocking to add an element of surprise and intrigue. The giver can choose to reveal themselves or keep the mystery alive. This twist not only makes the stocking experience more memorable but also encourages thoughtful gift-giving.

6. The Stocking Opening Ritual

The Hartleys had a special ritual for opening their stockings on Christmas morning. They gathered in the living room, still in their pajamas, with mugs of hot chocolate in hand. They took turns pulling out items from their stockings, savoring each discovery and sharing laughs and thanks.

"Look, I got a new journal!" Mrs. Hartley said, holding up a beautifully bound book. "Perfect for starting the new year."

Mr. Hartley pulled out a small jar of Mrs. Hartley's homemade strawberry jam and grinned. "Breakfast just got a whole lot sweeter."

Each stocking revealed small delights that brought smiles and warmth, underscoring the joy that can be found in the little things.

Activity Tip: Create a ritual around the stocking-opening experience. Encourage each person to take turns, savoring the moment and expressing gratitude for each item. This practice transforms the process into a meaningful, shared experience that highlights the thoughtfulness of each gift.

The Heart of the Perfect Stocking

The magic of the perfect stocking lies not in the size or cost of its contents but in the care and thoughtfulness that go into filling it. The stocking tells a story, reflecting the personality, needs, and loves of the recipient. Through the process of crafting, hunting, and filling the stockings, families can create memories that last a lifetime.

The tradition of stocking stuffing is a celebration of the small, the meaningful, and the whimsical. It embodies the spirit of Christmas—finding joy in giving, delight in surprise, and warmth in togetherness. As you hang your stockings this year, let your creativity and thoughtfulness guide you, and may your efforts fill your home with the true magic of the season.

Chapter 28: Winter Wonderland Crafts

Creating handmade Christmas decorations is a cherished holiday tradition that brings warmth and creativity to the season. Whether you're crafting alone, with friends, or as a family, these winter-themed projects allow you to personalize your holiday décor while infusing your home with the magic of the season. In this chapter, you'll discover a collection of *Winter Wonderland Crafts,* each with a story to enrich the experience and make the decorations even more special. These crafts range from simple projects for children to more intricate designs for experienced crafters, all meant to add a touch of handmade magic to your Christmas celebrations.

1. Snowy Pinecone Elves

The Story Behind the Craft: In the quaint village of Frostwood, the legend of the *Pinecone Elves* is a tale passed down through generations. It is said that these tiny, magical elves live deep in the pine forests and emerge only during the Christmas season. They sprinkle the woods with frost and guide travelers through the snow, their pinecone hats glistening under the moonlight. To honor these cheerful little creatures, villagers would make their own pinecone elves as decorations, believing they would bring good fortune and joy to their homes.

Craft Materials:

- Pinecones
- Small wooden beads (for the head)
- Felt (in various colors) for the hat and scarf
- Hot glue gun
- Paint (optional)
- Small twigs (for arms)
- String (for hanging)

Instructions:

1. Start by choosing a pinecone that will serve as the body of your elf. Clean off any dirt and debris.
2. Glue a small wooden bead to the top of the pinecone to create the head. You can paint a simple face on the bead with a tiny brush or marker.
3. Cut a triangle out of the felt to create a hat. Wrap it into a cone shape and glue it onto the bead. For an extra touch, glue a small pom-pom to the tip of the hat.
4. Cut a small strip of felt to make a scarf. Wrap it around the "neck" of the elf, securing it with a dab of glue.
5. Attach two small twigs to the sides of the pinecone using glue to create arms.
6. If you'd like to hang your pinecone elf, attach a piece of string to the top of the hat.

Display Tip: These adorable pinecone elves look perfect nestled in a wreath, hung on the Christmas tree, or scattered across the mantelpiece. As you create them, imagine the cheerful elves of Frostwood bringing their wintry magic into your home.

2. Crystal Snowflake Ornaments

The Story Behind the Craft: In the northern town of Glimmermere, children would watch the snowfall each Christmas Eve, marveling at the intricate designs of the snowflakes that covered the world in white. Legend has it that each snowflake was crafted by a frost fairy, and the most beautiful ones were captured by the townsfolk in crystal ornaments to preserve their magic through the year. This craft captures the beauty of those snowflakes, allowing you to hang your own frosty wonders on your tree.

Craft Materials:

- White pipe cleaners
- Scissors
- String
- Borax powder
- Boiling water
- Large glass jars or containers
- Food coloring (optional)

Instructions:

1. Cut the pipe cleaners into three equal pieces. Twist them together at the center to form a six-pointed star shape, mimicking a snowflake's natural symmetry.
2. Attach a piece of string to one point of the snowflake and tie the other end to a pencil or chopstick.
3. Fill a large glass jar with boiling water, leaving some space at the top. Add borax powder, one tablespoon at a time, stirring until it dissolves. You'll need about three tablespoons of borax for each cup of water. If you'd like colored snowflakes, add a few drops of food coloring.

4. Lower the snowflake into the jar, making sure it is completely submerged and not touching the sides or bottom. Rest the pencil across the top of the jar.
5. Leave the jar in a cool, undisturbed place overnight. As the water cools, borax crystals will form on the pipe cleaner, creating a sparkling snowflake.
6. Carefully remove the snowflake from the jar and let it dry.

Display Tip: These crystal snowflakes make stunning ornaments for your tree or window decorations. Share the story of Glimmermere with friends and family as they admire your frosty creations.

3. Cinnamon Stick Candle Holders

The Story Behind the Craft: In ancient winter festivals, candles were symbols of hope and light, warding off the darkness of the long nights. To bring the warmth of these traditions into their homes, families in the village of Hearthwood would decorate candles with fragrant cinnamon sticks, infusing their spaces with the comforting scent of spice. Making these candle holders is a way to carry on this tradition, filling your home with light and warmth.

Craft Materials:

- Small pillar candles (white or red work best)
- Cinnamon sticks
- Hot glue gun
- Ribbon or twine
- Optional: evergreen sprigs, dried orange slices, or star anise for extra decoration

Instructions:

1. Place the candle on a flat surface. Select cinnamon sticks of similar length for a uniform appearance.
2. One at a time, glue the cinnamon sticks vertically around the candle, pressing them close together until the candle is fully surrounded.
3. Once the cinnamon sticks are securely attached, wrap a ribbon or twine around the middle of the candle to add a decorative touch. For an extra festive look, tuck in a sprig of evergreen or a dried orange slice.
4. Let the glue dry completely before using the candle holder.

Safety Tip: Place a candle inside a clear glass holder before lighting it to ensure the flame stays safely away from the cinnamon sticks.

Display Tip: These candle holders make perfect centerpieces for your holiday table. Light them during a cozy evening to fill the room with a warm, spicy fragrance, telling the tale of Hearthwood and its traditions.

4. Woodland Creature Ornaments

The Story Behind the Craft: According to forest folklore, woodland creatures gather each winter to celebrate the turning of the season. They adorn their homes with bits of moss, berries, and fallen leaves, making the forest glow with festive cheer. Inspired by this legend, creating woodland creature ornaments brings a touch of nature and whimsy to your Christmas tree.

Craft Materials:

- Felt (brown, white, grey, and other natural colors)
- Scissors
- Needle and thread (or hot glue for a quicker option)
- Cotton balls or stuffing
- Black beads or buttons (for eyes)
- Ribbon or string for hanging

Instructions:

1. Draw simple animal shapes (like a fox, owl, or deer) onto the felt and cut out two identical pieces for each ornament.
2. Place the two felt pieces together and sew around the edges, leaving a small opening. Alternatively, use hot glue to attach the edges. Stuff the ornament lightly with cotton balls or stuffing before sealing the opening.
3. Sew or glue on black beads for eyes and additional felt pieces for details, such as ears, tails, or wings.
4. Attach a loop of ribbon or string to the top of the ornament for hanging.

Display Tip: Create a forest-themed corner on your tree, hanging your felt creatures among pinecones and small sprigs of greenery. Share the story of the woodland creatures with your guests, inviting them into the magic of the forest's winter celebration.

5. Sparkling Snow Globe Jars

The Story Behind the Craft: In the enchanted town of Wintervale, it is said that every snow globe holds a piece of winter's magic, capturing the beauty of snowfalls and frost-kissed mornings. Families in Wintervale would create their own snow globes, believing that each one could grant a wish when shaken on Christmas Eve.

Craft Materials:

- Clear glass jars with lids (mason jars work well)
- Small holiday figurines (such as miniature trees, deer, or snowmen)
- Waterproof glue
- Distilled water
- Glycerin (to make the snow float more slowly)
- Glitter (silver, white, or iridescent)
- Optional: small beads or snowflake confetti

Instructions:

1. Remove the lid from the jar and glue your figurine to the inside of the lid. Allow the glue to dry completely.
2. Fill the jar with distilled water, leaving a small gap at the top.
3. Add a few drops of glycerin to the water to help the glitter float slowly. Sprinkle in a generous amount of glitter and, if desired, small beads or snowflake confetti.
4. Apply a line of waterproof glue around the inner edge of the lid, then carefully screw it onto the jar to seal it.
5. Turn the jar upside down and give it a gentle shake to see the snow swirl around your winter scene.

Display Tip: Arrange your snow globe jars on a mantel or windowsill, telling the story of Wintervale and its wish-granting snow globes. Invite family and friends to shake the globes and make a wish, adding a touch of wonder to your holiday decor.

Crafting Your Winter Wonderland

Each craft in this chapter brings its own story and charm, transforming your home into a winter wonderland filled with handmade magic. Whether you're creating pinecone elves that embody the spirit of the forest, candle holders that fill your space with warmth, or snow globes that capture the beauty of winter, these crafts invite you to weave your own holiday traditions into every detail.

As you work on these projects, share the stories behind each creation with your family and friends. Let them become a part of your holiday narrative, infusing your decorations with meaning and a touch of the season's enchantment. With these crafts, you can celebrate the beauty of winter and the joy of creating together, turning your home into a place where Christmas magic truly shines.

Chapter 29: The Christmas Pageant

In the heart of the cozy village of Maple Hollow, nestled amidst snow-covered hills and towering evergreens, preparations for the annual *Christmas Pageant* were in full swing. The pageant was a cherished tradition, not just a performance, but a celebration of community, unity, and the magic of Christmas. Every year, villagers of all ages came together to create something beautiful, a reminder that Christmas was not only about gifts and decorations, but about the warmth of togetherness.

This year, the pageant would be extra special, for it marked the 50th anniversary of this beloved tradition. As the story of the village's Christmas play unfolds, you'll witness the joy, challenges, and triumphs that bring a community closer, highlighting the true spirit of the season.

The Origins of the Maple Hollow Christmas Pageant

Fifty years ago, the village of Maple Hollow had been a small, quiet place, where winters could feel long and lonely. One particularly harsh winter, the villagers found themselves struggling with the cold and dark. To lift everyone's spirits, a group of villagers decided to organize a small play in the town square on Christmas Eve.

It wasn't a grand affair—just a few simple costumes, a makeshift stage, and some candlelight. But as the villagers gathered to watch and participate, laughter filled the air, and the warmth of togetherness melted away the chill of winter. The pageant brought smiles, cheers, and tears of joy. From that day forward, the Christmas Pageant became an annual event, growing more vibrant with each passing year, weaving itself into the fabric of Maple Hollow's Christmas traditions.

Preparations Begin: The Spirit of Participation

As the 50th anniversary approached, the entire village buzzed with excitement. Preparations began in earnest at the start of December. In Maple Hollow, everyone had a role to play, from the youngest child to the oldest grandparent. This year, the pageant would tell the story of the *Christmas Star,* a tale passed down through generations about a star that guided villagers to a place of hope and unity.

1. The Town Meeting: Choosing Roles and Responsibilities

On a crisp December evening, the townspeople gathered in the village hall for the first pageant meeting. Mrs. Pembroke, a spirited woman who had directed the pageant for the past twenty years, stood at the front of the room with a clipboard in hand.

"Welcome, everyone!" she called out, her voice filled with warmth. "This year's pageant is going to be our best yet. It's a celebration of fifty years of community and Christmas joy. Now, let's start by assigning roles."

The room was abuzz with chatter as volunteers came forward. Little Timmy raised his hand eagerly, his eyes shining. "I want to be the Star!" he exclaimed, referring to the main character, a guiding star that leads the story's travelers to the heart of Christmas.

Mrs. Pembroke smiled and nodded. "The Star it is, Timmy. Now, we'll need shepherds, travelers, and carolers. And of course, we need help with costumes, set design, and baking for the Christmas market."

Hands shot up across the room as villagers offered their help. Mrs. Whitley, known for her sewing skills, volunteered to make the costumes. The baker, Mr. Jensen, promised to supply cookies and hot cider for the market stalls. Even Mr. Griggs, who usually kept to himself, offered to help build the stage.

Community Tip: In planning a Christmas pageant or community event, involve as many people as possible. Allowing everyone to contribute in their own way not only lightens the workload but fosters a sense of shared purpose and joy.

2. Rehearsals: The Joy of Coming Together

In the weeks leading up to Christmas Eve, the village hall became a hub of activity. Rehearsals were held twice a week, filling the hall with laughter, music, and the clatter of costumes and props. The children practiced their lines with enthusiasm, while the adults helped with set changes and lighting.

Timmy, in his role as the Star, practiced guiding the other characters—shepherds, villagers, and travelers—through the forest to the center of the stage, where a simple manger was set. He took his role seriously, often reminding the others of their places and lines with a sense of responsibility that made the adults chuckle.

"Don't forget to follow the Star!" Timmy would call out, his voice earnest and clear. The other children and adults, playing their parts, would smile and follow his lead, knowing that he embodied the spirit of hope and guidance that the story represented.

In another corner, Mrs. Whitley busily stitched costumes, transforming simple fabrics into robes, cloaks, and crowns. "These will look wonderful under the stage lights," she said proudly, holding up a shimmering blue cloak for Timmy's Star costume.

As rehearsals continued, the villagers grew closer, sharing stories, laughter, and the occasional mishap. One evening, as they practiced in the hall, a gust of wind blew through the open window, scattering props and causing a moment of chaos. The villagers laughed as they scrambled to gather everything back up, with Mr. Griggs exclaiming, "Well, it wouldn't be a proper pageant without a bit of excitement!"

Community Tip: Rehearsals and preparations are about more than just perfecting the performance. They provide an opportunity to build connections, enjoy the process, and create memories that will last long after the event is over.

3. The Set Design: Creating a Winter Wonderland

In the village square, Mr. Griggs and his team of volunteers worked on building the stage. It would be set against the backdrop of the village Christmas tree, which was already decorated with twinkling lights and ornaments.

"We're going for a winter wonderland theme," Mr. Griggs explained as he hammered the last nail into the wooden frame. "Snow-covered trees, a glowing path, and lanterns to guide the travelers."

The children helped paint the scenery, transforming plywood into snowy forests and star-filled skies. Mrs. Pembroke supervised with a watchful eye, ensuring that each detail captured the magic of the story.

When the set was finally completed, it looked like a scene from a fairytale. The stage sparkled with artificial snow, while strings of lights crisscrossed overhead to mimic the stars. In the center was the humble manger, surrounded by lanterns and evergreen boughs. It was simple yet enchanting, embodying the wonder of the Christmas season.

Community Tip: When creating the set for a community play, involve both children and adults in the design process. Use simple materials like plywood, paint, and lights to create a scene that reflects the magic of the story you're telling.

4. The Christmas Eve Pageant: A Night of Magic

At last, Christmas Eve arrived. The villagers gathered in the square, wrapped in warm coats and scarves, their breath misting in the cold air. The scent of mulled cider and baked goods filled the air as market stalls lined the edge of the square, adding to the festive atmosphere.

The lights dimmed, and a hush fell over the crowd as the pageant began. The children, dressed in their costumes, took to the stage, their faces glowing with excitement and a touch of nervousness. Timmy, standing at the front as the Star, raised his arms and began to speak.

"Follow the Star," he intoned, his voice steady and clear, "for it will guide you to the heart of Christmas."

As the other characters moved across the stage, guided by Timmy's Star, the audience watched in rapt attention. The story unfolded through music, dialogue, and song, telling of travelers who, lost in the winter woods, find their way to a place of warmth, light, and love. Along the journey, they discover that the true spirit of Christmas lies not in grand gifts or feasts, but in kindness, sharing, and the bonds they form along the way.

When the final scene arrived, the villagers gathered around the manger, singing a carol that filled the square with harmony and warmth. Timmy, as the Star, stood at the center, his face shining with pride and joy.

As the last note faded, the audience erupted into applause. Mrs. Pembroke, tears in her eyes, stepped forward. "Thank you, everyone, for making this year's pageant so special," she said, her voice trembling with emotion. "Fifty years of bringing our community together—here's to fifty more."

Community Tip: A Christmas pageant is more than just a performance; it is a celebration of community spirit. Whether it's through music, storytelling, or shared effort, the pageant brings people together, creating a tradition that resonates with the heart of Christmas.

5. Celebrating After the Show: The True Spirit of Christmas

After the pageant, the villagers gathered around the market stalls for hot cocoa, cider, and freshly baked cookies. The children ran through the snow, laughing and chasing each other, while the adults shared stories and embraced.

Timmy stood with his parents, holding a cup of cocoa, his eyes still sparkling from the excitement of the performance. "Did I do a good job, Mom?" he asked, looking up at his mother.

Mrs. Hartley knelt down and hugged him. "You were the best Star the village has ever seen," she said warmly. "You guided everyone to the heart of Christmas, just like the story."

As the evening wore on, the villagers joined hands and sang carols beneath the stars, their voices rising in harmony against the stillness of the night. In that moment, they felt the true magic of Christmas—the joy of togetherness, the warmth of shared tradition, and the light

Chapter 30: The Great Snowball Fight

The village of Maple Hollow had many cherished Christmas traditions, but perhaps none was more eagerly anticipated by the children than the *Great Snowball Fight.* Each year, on the day after Christmas, the villagers gathered for an epic battle of laughter, skill, and strategy. This event was more than just playful competition; it was a celebration of the simple joys of winter and the camaraderie that comes from being part of a close-knit community. As the tale of this year's snowball fight unfolds, you'll also find helpful tips on how to host your own, ensuring it becomes a beloved tradition for years to come.

The Morning of the Snowball Fight: A Winter Wonderland

It was early morning on December 26th when the first flakes began to fall, creating a blanket of fresh, powdery snow across Maple Hollow. The children woke to the sight of a perfect winter wonderland outside their windows, squealing with excitement. Snowball Fight Day had arrived!

In the town square, Mr. Griggs and Mrs. Pembroke, the organizers of the event, were already busy preparing for the battle. They laid out the boundaries, set up snow forts for each team, and placed markers for the neutral zones. A large banner strung across the square read: *"Welcome to the Great Snowball Fight!"*

Hosting Tip: Choose an open area, such as a park or backyard, for your snowball fight. Mark off boundaries using ropes, flags, or cones, and establish neutral zones where players can rest or collect snow. If possible, set up snow forts using piles of snow for each team to start with.

1. The Teams: Choosing Sides and Building Forts

By mid-morning, villagers of all ages gathered in the square, bundled in coats, hats, scarves, and mittens. The air was filled with laughter and the crunch of boots on the fresh snow. Excitement buzzed as they formed two teams: the *Snow Foxes* and the *Frost Wolves*.

The team captains—Timmy for the Snow Foxes and Sarah for the Frost Wolves—stood proudly at the front, waving to their teammates. The villagers lined up behind them, eager to start building their defenses.

"Alright, everyone!" Mr. Griggs called out, holding up a whistle. "You have thirty minutes to build your forts and prepare your snowballs. May the best team win!"

The square erupted into organized chaos as the teams got to work. Using shovels, buckets, and their gloved hands, they shaped walls and battlements out of the snow, creating fortresses that would serve as their bases during the fight. Each fort was unique, reflecting the creativity and spirit of its builders. The Snow Foxes' fort featured tall walls with small peep holes for throwing snowballs, while the Frost Wolves built a curved wall with a hidden tunnel for sneak attacks.

Hosting Tip: Give each team a set amount of time to build their forts before the fight begins. Provide simple tools like shovels, buckets, and sticks for shaping the snow. Encourage creativity, but set some ground rules to keep the forts safe and fair, such as limiting the height or thickness of the walls.

2. Preparing the Arsenal: The Art of Snowball Making

Once the forts were complete, it was time to prepare the snowballs. The teams spread out within their zones, gathering snow and packing it into balls. The air was filled with the sound of crunching snow and the sight of flying flakes.

Timmy, the Snow Fox captain, knelt beside his teammates, showing them the technique for making the perfect snowball. "You have to pack it tight, but not too hard," he instructed, shaping the snow into a ball in his mittens. "It should be firm enough to hold together but soft enough not to hurt when it hits."

Meanwhile, Sarah led the Frost Wolves in stockpiling snowballs behind their fort, arranging them in piles for easy access during the battle. They even created a few "special" snowballs—larger ones packed loosely to create a shower of snow on impact.

Hosting Tip: Set guidelines for snowball size and consistency to ensure safety. Snowballs should be about the size of a tennis ball and packed loosely enough to break apart on impact. For younger children, consider providing a demonstration of how to make safe, soft snowballs.

3. The Battle Begins: Strategies and Fun

With forts built and snowballs ready, Mr. Griggs blew the whistle to signal the start of the fight. A cheer went up from both teams, and the air was suddenly filled with flying snowballs. The sound of laughter, shouts, and the occasional "Gotcha!" echoed across the square.

The Snow Foxes adopted a defensive strategy, using their fort's tall walls to hide behind and pop up for surprise attacks. Timmy led his team with enthusiasm, calling out, "Ready... aim... fire!" as snowballs sailed over the fort's walls toward the Frost Wolves.

On the other side, the Frost Wolves took a more aggressive approach. Sarah coordinated her team's movements, sending small squads to flank the Snow Foxes and launch a flurry of snowballs from different angles.

They used their fort's tunnel to sneak out and launch surprise attacks before retreating to safety.

The battle raged for what felt like hours, with players diving, dodging, and launching snowballs with joyful abandon. Snowballs whizzed through the air, some landing with satisfying *plops* while others exploded in clouds of powder. The village square transformed into a scene of organized chaos, with both teams fighting valiantly yet playfully.

Hosting Tip: Introduce simple rules to keep the game safe and enjoyable. For example, designate out-of-bounds areas, set time limits for rounds, and enforce "no headshots" to prevent accidents. Encourage a mix of strategies—defensive fort-building, offensive flanking, and surprise tactics—to keep the game dynamic and fun.

4. The Ceasefire: Time to Warm Up

As the sun climbed higher in the sky and cheeks grew rosy from the cold, Mr. Griggs blew his whistle again. "Ceasefire!" he called out, signaling a break in the action. Both teams lowered their snowballs and exchanged grins, their breath misting in the cold air.

Mrs. Pembroke brought out a large thermos of hot cocoa and cups, and the players gathered in the neutral zone to warm up. Hands clasped around steaming mugs, they laughed and swapped stories about the best throws and most daring maneuvers of the fight so far.

"Did you see that curveball from Luke?" Timmy exclaimed, shaking his head in admiration. "I thought I was safe behind the wall!"

Sarah grinned, wiping snow from her jacket. "We've got some tricks up our sleeves for the next round," she teased, raising her cup in a mock toast to Timmy. "May the best team win!"

Hosting Tip: Schedule breaks during the snowball fight for warming up and hydrating. Serve hot drinks like cocoa or cider, and provide a sheltered area where participants can take a breather. This not only ensures safety in the cold weather but also gives everyone a chance to share stories and bond.

5. The Final Round: Declaring a Winner

After the break, it was time for the final round. The teams returned to their forts with renewed energy, ready to give it their all. Snowballs flew faster and more furiously than before, each side pushing to gain the upper hand.

In a daring move, Timmy led a charge from the Snow Foxes, sprinting across the neutral zone with a snowball in each hand. The Frost Wolves countered with a volley of snowballs, sending the Snow Foxes scrambling for cover. The square was filled with laughter and the shouts of excited players, as each team made one last effort to secure victory.

Finally, as the sun began to dip toward the horizon, Mr. Griggs blew the whistle three times, signaling the end of the fight. Both teams cheered, raising their hands in victory.

"Gather 'round, everyone!" Mrs. Pembroke called out, holding up a ribboned wreath. "After much deliberation, we declare this year's Great Snowball Fight a draw!"

The announcement was met with laughter and applause. The villagers, faces flushed and eyes shining, embraced one another. It didn't matter who had won; what mattered was the joy, fun, and sense of community they had shared.

Hosting Tip: When declaring the end of the snowball fight, consider declaring all participants as winners to emphasize the fun and camaraderie of the event. If you do decide to have a competitive element, offer playful awards or titles, such as "Best Snowball Thrower" or "Most Creative Fort."

The Aftermath: Celebrating Togetherness

With the fight over, the villagers gathered for a post-battle celebration. A bonfire was lit in the square, where they roasted marshmallows and shared stories of the day's highlights. The air was filled with the sound of laughter and the warmth of friendship.

Timmy and Sarah, now arm-in-arm, stood by the fire with their teammates. "That was the best snowball fight ever!" Timmy declared, his eyes sparkling. "I can't wait to do it again next year."

"Me too," Sarah agreed, raising her marshmallow stick. "Here's to the Great Snowball Fight, and to the best team—both of us!"

Everyone raised their mugs and sticks in a cheer, celebrating not just the battle, but the joy of coming together for a day of fun in the snow.

Hosting Tip: Conclude the snowball fight with a gathering around a fire or table of treats. Sharing hot food, drinks, and stories provides a warm and festive ending to the event, leaving everyone with fond memories of the day.

Bringing the Great Snowball Fight to Life

The Great Snowball Fight of Maple Hollow is more than just a game; it is a celebration of winter, friendship, and the simple joy of playing together in the snow. Hosting your own snowball fight can be a wonderful way to bring people together, fostering laughter, teamwork, and a touch of friendly competition.

As you gather your friends and family for your own snowball battle, remember the heart of the tradition: it's not about who wins or loses, but about the fun and warmth of spending time with others. So, pack those snowballs, build those forts, and let the laughter fill the air—because nothing captures the spirit of winter quite like a good-natured snowball fight!

Part 7: *The Magic Within: Finding Christmas Spirit*

Chapter 31: The Spirit of Giving

The holiday season is a time filled with joy, warmth, and togetherness, but it is also a reminder of the importance of *giving*. Beyond the gifts exchanged between family and friends, Christmas invites us to extend kindness, generosity, and compassion to those in need. This chapter delves into the heartwarming narratives of charitable acts and explores creative ways to give back during the holiday season. By sharing these stories, we hope to inspire you to embrace the *spirit of giving* and make a positive impact in your community.

1. The Christmas Feast: Feeding the Hungry

In the small village of North Haven, the townsfolk came together each year for a special Christmas feast, an event that had become known as the *Christmas Table*. It began decades ago when an elderly woman named Mrs. Thornton, known for her generosity and warm heart, noticed that some of her neighbors were struggling to put food on the table during the winter months.

One Christmas Eve, she decided to open her home to anyone who needed a warm meal. She spent the day cooking hearty stews, baking bread, and preparing pies with the help of her neighbors. That evening, her house was filled with the aroma of freshly baked goods and the laughter of people from all walks of life. It was a humble gathering, but it radiated warmth and goodwill. From that night on, the Christmas Table became a village tradition, growing larger each year.

Now, every Christmas, the villagers of North Haven transform the town hall into a bustling dining hall. Families cook dishes to share, volunteers set up tables, and local musicians provide festive music. It is a day of unity, where everyone, regardless of their circumstances, comes together to celebrate the season over a warm, communal meal.

How to Give Back: Host a holiday meal for those in need, either in your home, at a community center, or in partnership with a local charity. If hosting a meal isn't feasible, consider donating food to a local food bank or volunteering to serve meals at a soup kitchen. Providing nourishment and company can be a deeply meaningful way to embody the spirit of giving.

2. The Christmas Blanket Drive: Warming the Winter

In the city of Ashton, winters were particularly harsh, with biting winds and heavy snowfall. Many people struggled to stay warm, especially those without permanent homes. Moved by the plight of the less fortunate, a group of schoolchildren decided to start a *Christmas Blanket Drive* one year.

Led by their teacher, Mr. Anderson, the children began collecting blankets, coats, gloves, and scarves to distribute to those in need. They visited neighbors, local businesses, and even set up a stall at the Christmas market to spread the word. Donations poured in, filling their classroom with piles of warm, cozy blankets.

On Christmas Eve, the children, along with their parents and Mr. Anderson, loaded the blankets into a van and drove to the city's shelters. As they handed out the blankets, they saw the faces of the recipients light up, not just from the warmth of the gifts, but from the kindness behind them. The experience left an indelible mark on the children, teaching them that even the smallest acts of giving could make a world of difference.

How to Give Back: Organize a blanket, coat, or winter clothing drive in your community. Reach out to friends, family, and local businesses for donations. Once collected, distribute the items to homeless shelters, community centers, or directly to those in need. Such drives are especially impactful during the colder months, providing both warmth and a reminder that people care.

3. The Gift of Music: Bringing Joy to the Lonely

In Maple Hollow, a tradition known as the *Yuletide Serenade* had brought joy to the community for generations. It started with a young musician named Emily, who had moved to the village to escape the hustle of the city. One Christmas, she learned that many elderly residents in the village's care home were feeling lonely during the holidays. Wanting to spread some cheer, Emily gathered a group of friends and set out with their instruments to perform carols for the residents.

As the music filled the halls, the residents' faces lit up. Some sang along, while others simply closed their eyes and swayed to the melodies. The simple act of sharing music brought the room to life, transforming it from a place of solitude to one of joy and warmth. Since that night, the Yuletide Serenade has become an annual tradition in Maple Hollow, with musicians of all ages volunteering to visit care homes, hospitals, and community centers to share the gift of music.

How to Give Back: Share your talents by visiting care homes, hospitals, or shelters to perform music, read stories, or engage in conversation with residents. Acts of kindness like singing carols, playing instruments, or even sharing holiday stories can lift the spirits of those who might feel isolated or lonely during the holidays.

4. The Secret Santa: Anonymous Acts of Kindness

In the bustling city of Elmford, a mysterious figure known as the *Secret Santa* had been spreading cheer every Christmas for years. No one knew who he or she was, but each December, families in need would find unexpected gifts on their doorsteps: boxes of groceries, warm clothing, toys for children, and notes of encouragement.

One year, the Smith family, who had been struggling after Mr. Smith lost his job, received a package filled with groceries, a warm blanket, and a card that read, "You are not alone. Merry Christmas." It was a small gesture, but it filled their home with hope and light during a difficult time. Stories of the Secret Santa's generosity began to circulate, inspiring others to pay the kindness forward in their own ways.

Inspired by the anonymous acts of the Secret Santa, other Elmford residents began participating in similar efforts. Some would leave small gifts in their neighbors' mailboxes, others would pay for a stranger's coffee or groceries, and some donated toys and necessities to local charities in the spirit of giving without recognition.

How to Give Back: Become a "Secret Santa" in your community. Leave small gifts or essential items anonymously for those who may need a lift in spirits during the holiday season. You can also donate to toy drives, pay for someone's meal, or contribute to holiday funds at local schools, hospitals, or community centers. The act of giving, done without expectation of recognition, truly embodies the selflessness of the season.

5. The Christmas Wish Tree: Granting Holiday Wishes

In the town square of Riverton stood a grand evergreen, known as the *Christmas Wish Tree*. Each December, the tree was adorned not only with lights and ornaments but also with hundreds of tags bearing holiday wishes. The tradition began when the Riverton Community Center started collecting wishes from children and families in need, writing them on tags that were then hung on the tree.

Villagers and visitors would stop by, read the tags, and select one or more wishes to fulfill. Some wishes were simple, like a new pair of mittens or a toy train, while others were more personal, such as a grocery gift card for a struggling family or a warm coat for an elderly neighbor.

One year, a little girl named Ava wished for a set of art supplies to pursue her dream of becoming an artist. When she found a beautifully wrapped package on her doorstep with a note that said, "May your creativity shine bright," her eyes sparkled with happiness. Ava's story, like many others, became a testament to the power of community and the joy that comes from making wishes come true.

How to Give Back: Start a "Wish Tree" in your community, workplace, or school. Collect wishes from individuals or families in need and place them on the tree for others to fulfill. This activity fosters a sense of connection and provides a tangible way for people to contribute directly to making someone's holiday a little brighter.

6. Making Time for Giving: Volunteering with Heart

In the city of Rosewood, the holiday season was marked by the tireless efforts of volunteers at the *Hope Shelter*. Each year, residents of all ages dedicated time to serving meals, organizing clothing drives, and setting up a special Christmas Eve dinner for those without homes or family to share the holiday with.

Among the volunteers was Mrs. Clark, a retired teacher who had made it her mission to spend the month of December helping others. She organized activities for the shelter's residents, including crafts, storytelling sessions, and a holiday card-making workshop. The cards were then sent to soldiers overseas, patients in hospitals, and seniors in care homes, spreading the warmth of the season far and wide.

"Giving your time is the most precious gift of all," Mrs. Clark often said. "A smile, a meal, a helping hand—these acts create ripples of kindness that can change lives."

How to Give Back: Dedicate time to volunteer at a shelter, food bank, or community center. Whether it's serving meals, organizing donations, or simply offering companionship, volunteering embodies the essence of the season. Look for local organizations that need extra hands during the holidays and consider involving friends or family to share the experience.

The Spirit of Giving: Spreading Kindness Throughout the Year

These stories remind us that the spirit of giving goes beyond gifts wrapped in shiny paper. It is found in the shared meal, the warm blanket, the kind word, and the time spent with others. Giving is about extending a hand to those in need, offering comfort, joy, and a reminder that no one is ever truly alone.

As you celebrate this holiday season, consider how you can bring light into the lives of others. Whether it's through a small act of kindness or a larger charitable effort, each gesture contributes to the tapestry of compassion that defines Christmas. By embracing the spirit of giving, you become part of a tradition that enriches not only the lives of others but your own as well.

So, as you hang your stockings, decorate your tree, and prepare your feasts, take a moment to think about the ways you can give back. For it is in giving that we find the true magic of the season—a magic that lasts far beyond Christmas Day, leaving a legacy of love and generosity for the year to come.

Chapter 32: The Forgotten Ornament

Snow fell gently over the village of Hearthstead, blanketing the rooftops and turning the town square into a winter wonderland. Christmas was just days away, and the excitement was palpable. Families busily decorated their homes, filled their kitchens with the scent of baked goods, and shared laughter as they prepared for the season's festivities. In one small house near the edge of the village, the Linwood family was getting ready to decorate their Christmas tree. This year, however, would be different, for they were about to rediscover a lost treasure—the *Forgotten Ornament*—and, in doing so, rekindle the true meaning of Christmas.

The Linwood Family's Christmas Routine

The Linwoods had a cherished tradition of decorating the Christmas tree on the weekend before Christmas. The day began with a family trip to the local tree farm to pick out the perfect pine. Every year, they selected a tree that was just the right height to touch the living room ceiling and full enough to carry the weight of their many ornaments. This year was no exception.

"Found it!" exclaimed Peter, the eldest of the Linwood children, as he pointed to a tall, perfectly shaped pine. His siblings, Lily and Emma, ran over, clapping their hands in agreement.

Mr. and Mrs. Linwood smiled and nodded. "Looks like we have a winner," Mr. Linwood said, his voice filled with warmth. With the tree tied to the top of their car, they made their way back home, ready to transform their living room into a holiday haven.

Once inside, the family set up the tree in the corner of the room and began unpacking boxes of ornaments. As always, they took their time, carefully unwrapping each decoration and reminiscing about its history. There were hand-painted glass balls, wooden angels, and delicate stars. Some ornaments had been in the family for generations, while others were new additions from recent years.

Lily, the youngest, pulled out an ornament of a reindeer and held it up to the light. "Remember this one?" she asked, grinning. "It's from the year I learned to ski!"

Mrs. Linwood laughed. "That's right. You were so proud of that little reindeer because it reminded you of how brave you were."

The room filled with chatter and laughter as the family adorned the tree. Yet, amid all the joy, Mr. Linwood noticed something odd. "Wait a moment," he said, his brow furrowing as he rummaged through the bottom of the last box. "Where is the old star?"

The Search for the Old Ornament

The "old star" was a special ornament, a golden star with intricate carvings and a delicate shimmer that had adorned the top of the Linwood family tree for generations. It had belonged to Mr. Linwood's grandmother, who had passed it down to him as a symbol of family heritage and the light of Christmas. Every year, it was the crowning touch to their tree, signifying that the holiday preparations were complete.

"It should be here," Mrs. Linwood said, joining her husband in the search. "I'm sure we packed it away carefully last year."

The children gathered around, concerned expressions on their faces. "Did we lose it?" Emma asked, her voice tinged with worry. "Christmas won't feel the same without it."

They searched through the boxes, digging through tissue paper and tangled lights, but the star was nowhere to be found. A sense of sadness filled the room, casting a shadow over the festive spirit.

"Maybe we just misplaced it," Mr. Linwood said, trying to reassure his family. "Let's finish decorating for now. We'll look for it again later."

The family continued hanging ornaments, but the mood had shifted. The tree looked beautiful with its twinkling lights and colorful decorations, but something was missing. The star had always been more than just an ornament; it was a symbol of their family's shared memories and the light that Christmas brought into their lives.

Discovering the Forgotten Ornament

The following day, the Linwoods decided to check the attic, hoping that the star had been stored separately. As they climbed up into the dusty, dimly lit space, Mrs. Linwood spotted an old wooden chest tucked away in a corner.

"What's this?" she wondered aloud as she and Mr. Linwood carefully pulled the chest into the light. They lifted the lid, revealing a collection of forgotten items—books, keepsakes, and a few wrapped packages that looked decades old.

Lily's eyes widened. "It's like a treasure chest!"

As they sifted through the items, Mr. Linwood uncovered a small, worn-out box at the bottom. The lid was faded, but he recognized the family crest embossed on its surface. His hands trembled slightly as he opened the box, revealing a delicate, dust-covered ornament nestled inside.

"It's not the star," he murmured, lifting it out. "But I remember this..."

It was an old glass bauble, painted with a beautiful winter scene: a snow-covered village illuminated by a warm, glowing sky. Despite its age, it still shimmered softly, as if holding onto the light of many Christmases past.

"This was my grandmother's favorite ornament," Mr. Linwood explained, his voice filled with nostalgia. "She used to tell me that this bauble held the spirit of Christmas—the warmth, the love, and the joy of being together."

Lily reached out and touched the bauble. "It's beautiful," she whispered. "Why did we stop using it?"

Mr. Linwood thought for a moment. "I suppose it was set aside when we started using new decorations. Over time, it got buried and forgotten." He looked around at his family, seeing their faces softened by the story. "But maybe it's time we bring it back."

Bringing Back the Christmas Spirit

Back in the living room, the Linwoods gathered around the tree with the newly discovered bauble in hand. Carefully, they hung it in a prominent place near the top, where its painted village scene could be admired. As they stepped back, the room seemed to grow warmer, filled with a renewed sense of Christmas magic.

"It's perfect," Emma said, her eyes shining. "Even though we didn't find the star, this feels just right."

As the family stood together, gazing at the tree, Mr. Linwood spoke softly. "Christmas isn't about any one decoration or tradition. It's about the memories we make and the love we share. This bauble may have been forgotten, but its meaning hasn't changed. It reminds us that the spirit of Christmas is always here, as long as we carry it in our hearts."

The children nodded, feeling the truth of his words. In that moment, they realized that while ornaments and traditions were important, the real magic of Christmas came from the time spent together, the stories told, and the love that filled their home.

The Linwoods' New Tradition

From that year forward, the old bauble took its place on the Linwood family tree, not as a replacement for the star, but as a cherished reminder of their history and the enduring spirit of Christmas. They lovingly dubbed it *The Forgotten Ornament*, a symbol of how even the smallest, most overlooked things could hold immense meaning.

Each Christmas Eve, the Linwoods gathered around the tree to share stories about past holidays, the joy of giving, and the warmth of family. They would reflect on the year gone by and look forward to the year ahead, reminded by the bauble that the light of Christmas wasn't found in perfection, but in love and togetherness.

Lily, who had grown particularly fond of the bauble, suggested a new tradition: each year, the family would choose a different ornament that seemed "forgotten" or overlooked and give it a place of honor on the tree. This small act of recognition became a way to celebrate the beauty in all things, whether new or old, bright or faded.

The True Meaning of Christmas

The story of the Linwood family and the forgotten ornament teaches us that Christmas is not just about the outward decorations or the grandeur of holiday festivities. It is about the memories, the love, and the connections we share. Sometimes, in the rush of modern life, we may overlook or set aside the things that truly matter—much like the bauble that was once forgotten in a dusty attic.

Yet, when we take the time to rediscover and cherish these small treasures, we uncover the deeper meaning of Christmas. The forgotten ornament reminds us that the season's magic is not found in perfection or the newest trends but in the warmth of being together, the joy of shared stories, and the light that shines in each of us.

So, as you decorate your tree this year, take a moment to pause and reflect. Perhaps there is an old ornament tucked away, a piece of family history waiting to be rediscovered. Hang it on your tree, share its story, and let it serve as a reminder that the true spirit of Christmas is found in the love and joy that fills our hearts.

In the end, it is these small acts of remembering, cherishing, and sharing that keep the light of Christmas shining bright, year after year. And like the Linwood family, we learn that sometimes, it is in the forgotten things that we find the most profound meaning.

Chapter 33: The Book of Wishes

As the year draws to a close and Christmas fills the air with its magic, many of us find ourselves reflecting on the past year's joys, challenges, and growth. Amid the festivities, there is a quiet moment of anticipation for what the New Year will bring. This is the time for dreams, hopes, and wishes, and what better way to honor these feelings than to create a *Book of Wishes*? This chapter invites you to embark on an interactive journey, encouraging you to pause, reflect, and write down your wishes and aspirations for the year ahead.

The *Book of Wishes* is not just a simple list; it is a collection of your dreams, intentions, and the seeds you plant for the future. Whether you wish for personal growth, the well-being of loved ones, or positive changes in the world, putting your thoughts into words has a powerful way of setting them in motion. So, find a cozy spot, grab your favorite pen, and let's begin the journey into the Book of Wishes.

1. Preparing Your Book of Wishes

Before you start writing your wishes, take a moment to create a special place for them. The Book of Wishes can be anything you like—a beautiful journal, a handmade booklet, or even a collection of decorative notecards. What matters most is that it feels personal and meaningful to you. If you'd like, you can decorate the cover with elements that inspire you, such as stars, hearts, or images that represent your hopes for the coming year.

Materials to Gather:

- A journal, notebook, or a set of notecards
- Pens, markers, or colored pencils
- Stickers, washi tape, or small decorative items (optional)
- A quiet, comfortable space to reflect and write

Tip: If you're creating the Book of Wishes with family or friends, consider setting up a "wishing corner" with cozy blankets, fairy lights, and warm drinks to set the mood for introspection and sharing.

2. Reflecting on the Past Year

Before writing down your wishes for the New Year, it's helpful to reflect on the past year. This process is about recognizing what you have learned, what brought you joy, and what challenges you overcame. By acknowledging these experiences, you open the door to understanding what you truly wish for in the future.

Reflection Prompts:

- What moments brought you the most joy this year?
- What challenges did you face, and what did you learn from them?
- Who or what are you most grateful for?
- What was something new you tried this year, and how did it change you?

Take your time to ponder these questions. You may write your thoughts down in your Book of Wishes or simply keep them in mind as you move forward. Reflection helps ground you, providing clarity as you set your intentions for the New Year.

3. Writing Your Wishes: A Guided Journey

Now that you've reflected on the past, it's time to look ahead. In this part of the chapter, you'll find guided sections to help you organize your wishes into categories, covering various aspects of your life. Remember, wishes don't have to be grand or life-changing. They can be simple hopes, personal goals, or even dreams for the world. The act of writing them down is a powerful step toward making them a reality.

A. Wishes for Self-Growth

- In this section, focus on your personal development. What would you like to achieve, learn, or experience in the coming year? These wishes might include building new skills, exploring hobbies, improving health, or nurturing self-care practices.

- *Examples to Inspire You:*
    ◦ "I wish to take more time for self-care, finding moments of peace in each day."
    ◦ "I wish to learn a new language and explore its culture."
    ◦ "I wish to spend more time in nature, reconnecting with the world around me."

B. Wishes for Loved Ones

- This part of the Book of Wishes is dedicated to those you hold dear—family, friends, and even pets. What do you wish for their happiness, health, and success in the coming year?
- *Examples to Inspire You:*
    ◦ "I wish for my family to find joy in the little moments we share together."
    ◦ "I wish for my best friend to achieve her dreams and find the courage to pursue new adventures."
    ◦ "I wish for my pet to remain healthy and playful, bringing smiles to our home."

C. Wishes for the World

- Look beyond your immediate circle and consider what you hope for the world around you. These wishes might focus on the environment, global health, peace, or community support.
- *Examples to Inspire You:*
    ◦ "I wish for a world where kindness and compassion are shown to all creatures, great and small."
    ◦ "I wish for our planet to be cared for and protected, with efforts toward a more sustainable future."

- ◦ "I wish for unity and understanding among people, celebrating diversity and working together for common good."

D. Wishes for the Unknown

- Sometimes, we have wishes that are harder to define. They may be hopes for serendipity, unexpected opportunities, or simply a sense of wonder. This section is a space for those intangible desires.
- *Examples to Inspire You:*
    - ◦ "I wish for moments of unexpected joy that brighten even the most ordinary days."
    - ◦ "I wish to remain open to new experiences, embracing the unknown with curiosity."
    - ◦ "I wish to discover the magic in everyday life, no matter where I am."

Writing Exercise: Take a deep breath and let your thoughts flow onto the pages. Write freely, without judgment or concern for perfection. These wishes are yours, and they can be as varied and imaginative as you desire. Use colors, doodles, or symbols to illustrate your wishes if that resonates with you.

4. Rituals for the Book of Wishes

After you've completed your wishes, consider incorporating a ritual to honor and "activate" them. This can be a simple ceremony that adds a sense of magic and intention to your Book of Wishes.

A. The Candlelight Wish

- Find a quiet moment, preferably in the evening. Light a candle and place it near your Book of Wishes. As you open the book, take a moment to breathe deeply, feeling gratitude for the year past and hope for the year ahead. Gently read through each wish you've written, visualizing it coming to life. As you finish, close the book and blow out the candle, imagining the smoke carrying your wishes into the universe.

B. The Starry Night Wish

- If possible, take your Book of Wishes outside on a clear night. Find a place where you can see the stars, and open your book to a blank page. Spend a few moments gazing at the stars, letting your mind drift to the vastness of the sky. Write one final wish on the page, inspired by the beauty of the stars above. This wish can be anything—a hope for guidance, inspiration, or simply a reminder of the magic that exists in the world.

C. The Hidden Wish

- Write down one special wish on a small piece of paper. Fold it and tuck it into a secret pocket of your Book of Wishes or place it inside an envelope attached to the book's back cover. This hidden wish is something you keep private, a personal hope that holds special meaning for you. Promise yourself to revisit this wish at the end of the year to see how it has manifested or evolved.

5. Revisiting Your Wishes

The beauty of the Book of Wishes lies not only in the act of writing but also in revisiting your hopes as the year unfolds. Make a habit of opening the book at key moments—perhaps on the first day of spring, on a birthday, or during times of reflection. Use it as a reminder of the intentions you set and as a source of motivation and comfort.

Mid-Year Check-In: Around the halfway mark of the year, take a moment to revisit your wishes. Reflect on what has come to fruition, what has changed, and what new wishes have emerged. Use this opportunity to add new entries or modify existing ones, letting the book evolve with you.

6. Sharing and Connecting Through Wishes

While the Book of Wishes is a deeply personal endeavor, it can also be a way to connect with others. If you're creating it as a family, consider dedicating a few pages to collective wishes—hopes for family adventures, shared projects, or dreams for the community.

Gathering Idea: Host a "Wish Night" with family or friends. Gather together, light candles, and take turns reading a wish or two from your books. This practice fosters a sense of connection, support, and encouragement, reminding everyone that they are not alone in their dreams for the future.

The Power of the Book of Wishes

The *Book of Wishes* is more than just a collection of words; it is a reflection of your dreams, hopes, and the possibilities you envision for the future. By taking the time to write down your wishes, you acknowledge their importance, setting the stage for them to grow and take shape.

As you embark on this journey, remember that wishes are not about immediate results or perfection. They are expressions of your deepest desires and aspirations, reminding you to embrace the coming year with an open heart and a hopeful spirit.

So, go ahead—write your wishes, release them into the world, and trust that, in the beautiful dance of the universe, they will find their way to you in ways both expected and wonderfully surprising. With your *Book of Wishes* in hand, step into the New Year filled with the light, love, and infinite possibilities that the spirit of Christmas so generously offers.

Chapter 34: The Silent Gift

In the quaint, snow-covered village of Silverwood, nestled between rolling hills and dense pine forests, Christmas had always been a time of celebration and community. But this year, something extraordinary was about to happen—something that would touch every heart and become a legend whispered through the town for generations. It all began with an anonymous gift-giver, known simply as *The Silent Gift*, whose kindness and generosity would spread joy and hope throughout the village.

The Arrival of the First Gift

December had arrived, bringing with it crisp air and a blanket of snow that covered Silverwood's cobblestone streets. The villagers were busy preparing for the holidays, hanging wreaths on doors, stringing lights along rooftops, and setting up the grand Christmas tree in the town square. Yet, amidst the usual holiday hustle, an unexpected event set the town abuzz.

On the morning of December 1st, Mr. Hargrove, the postmaster, opened the door to the post office to begin his daily routine. There, on the steps, he found a small, neatly wrapped package tied with a simple red ribbon. No note, no name—only the word *"Joy"* scrawled across the top in elegant script.

Mr. Hargrove picked up the package, puzzled by its sudden appearance. "Who could have left this?" he wondered aloud, looking around the empty street. But there was no sign of anyone. With a mixture of curiosity and anticipation, he took the package inside and carefully unwrapped it.

Inside was a beautifully carved wooden ornament in the shape of a star, delicate and intricate, with a warm golden sheen. Alongside it was a smaller, handwritten note that read: *"To brighten your day and spread a little joy. Share it with the town."*

Touched by the gesture, Mr. Hargrove decided to hang the star on the post office door for all to see. By noon, news of the mysterious gift had spread through the village. People stopped by the post office to admire the star and speculate about its origins. "It must be from someone in town," they said. "But who could it be?"

The Gifts Continue

The next morning, a similar scene played out at the bakery. Mrs. Finch, the baker, arrived to find a small package on the doorstep, tied with the same red ribbon. Her heart skipped a beat as she knelt to pick it up, feeling the same curious wonder that had gripped Mr. Hargrove the day before.

Inside, she discovered a jar of homemade spiced jam, the aroma of cinnamon and cloves filling the air as she opened it. Accompanying the jar was a note: *"For the warmth you bring to our community with your kindness and bread."*

Mrs. Finch couldn't help but smile. She set the jar on the bakery counter, sharing its contents with customers throughout the day. "Whoever this Silent Gift is," she said to her regulars, "they have a heart full of Christmas spirit."

From that day forward, a new gift appeared each morning, left anonymously at a different place around the village. A basket of woolen scarves was found at the tailor's shop with a note that read: *"To wrap you in warmth this winter."* At the schoolhouse, a box of art supplies was discovered, addressed to the children with the message: *"Create and color your dreams."* Even the old town bench in the square was adorned with a soft, hand-knitted blanket, inviting weary passersby to rest and be comforted.

The Speculation Begins

The villagers were enchanted by this mystery. Each morning brought new excitement as they eagerly awaited the next gift and guessed who might be behind these acts of kindness.

"It must be old Mr. Thomas," some said, referring to the retired carpenter known for his quiet generosity.

"No, no," others argued. "It's probably Mrs. Harper, the schoolteacher. She's always doing things for the children."

Yet, no matter how much they speculated, no one could confirm the identity of the *Silent Gift*. The giver's anonymity only added to the magic, filling the town with a sense of wonder and community. Whoever it was, they clearly wanted to remain unknown, allowing their gifts to speak for themselves.

A Change in the Town's Heart

As the days passed, the gifts seemed to inspire the villagers to spread their own acts of kindness. Inspired by the Silent Gift's example, Mr. Hargrove began offering free postage for Christmas cards. Mrs. Finch baked extra loaves of bread each morning, handing them out to anyone in need. The tailor started stitching patches onto coats for those who couldn't afford new winter clothes.

The air in Silverwood grew warmer despite the cold, filled with a spirit of giving that flowed through every corner of the village. Strangers exchanged smiles on the street, and neighbors helped one another with shoveling snow or carrying firewood. The Silent Gift had sparked a chain reaction of generosity and goodwill, reminding everyone of the true meaning of Christmas.

The Final Gift: A Gift to the Whole Town

Christmas Eve arrived, and anticipation was at its peak. The townsfolk gathered in the square that morning, their breaths misting in the crisp air, eyes scanning the area for the final gift. They had come to expect that each gift carried a message of love, hope, or joy, and this day felt particularly special.

But as they waited, nothing appeared. The hours ticked by, and no package was found. The villagers exchanged puzzled glances. Had the Silent Gift decided to end their giving without a final message?

It wasn't until dusk that a child, little Clara, noticed something sparkling at the base of the grand Christmas tree in the square. "Look!" she cried, pointing. "There's something there!"

The villagers gathered around as Mr. Hargrove knelt to pick up a small, silver box nestled among the tree's roots. He opened it carefully, revealing a simple, shining key. Beside the key was a note that read: *"For the heart of Silverwood, with love. Find the door that this key unlocks."*

Confused yet intrigued, they looked around. What door could this key possibly open? Then, Mrs. Finch gasped and pointed toward the old community hall at the edge of the square. "The hall!" she exclaimed. "It's been locked for years since it fell into disrepair."

The townsfolk hurried to the hall, carrying lanterns to light their way. The building stood solemnly in the evening light, its windows dark and covered in frost. Mr. Hargrove approached the door and, with a trembling hand, inserted the key. It turned smoothly, and the door creaked open.

Inside, the hall was aglow with candles. Garlands hung from the rafters, and a large table was set in the center, laden with an assortment of food, drink, and a stack of gifts wrapped in simple brown paper. A large banner stretched across the room that read: *"Merry Christmas, Silverwood. The greatest gift is the joy of sharing."*

The villagers stood in awe, their hearts swelling with emotion. The Silent Gift had not just given them things; they had given the town back its gathering place, a place to come together, celebrate, and share the warmth of the season.

A Christmas Celebration of Sharing

That night, the hall was filled with laughter, music, and the sound of clinking glasses. The villagers brought what they could to add to the feast—Mrs. Finch's freshly baked bread, Mr. Hargrove's cider, the tailor's handmade decorations. They sang carols, shared stories, and exchanged the simple gifts left on the table.

As the evening wore on, the villagers no longer speculated about the identity of the Silent Gift. It no longer seemed to matter who they were. What mattered was the spirit they had spread throughout Silverwood—the spirit of giving without expectation, of joy in anonymity, of kindness that asked for nothing in return.

As the clock struck midnight, the villagers raised their glasses in a toast. "To the Silent Gift," Mr. Hargrove declared, "and to the spirit of Christmas that lives in all of us!"

The Legacy of the Silent Gift

From that year on, the story of the Silent Gift became a cherished legend in Silverwood. Every Christmas, the villagers would leave small, anonymous gifts around the town, not for recognition but to honor the tradition of giving for the sake of spreading joy. The community hall, now known as the *Silent Gift Hall*, became the heart of their Christmas celebrations, a symbol of the kindness that had brought them together.

And though the true identity of the original Silent Gift was never revealed, their legacy lived on in the generosity and love that filled Silverwood each holiday season. For the villagers had learned that the most precious gift was not something bought or wrapped, but the simple, quiet act of giving with an open heart.

The Spirit of the Silent Gift: As you finish this story, let it inspire you to embrace the spirit of the Silent Gift in your own way. Whether through a small, anonymous act of kindness or a thoughtful gesture shared with someone in need, you too can spread the light of Christmas. In the end, it is not the size of the gift but the heart behind it that truly makes it shine.

And so, with every silent gift you give, may you find joy in knowing that you are part of a greater story—a story of love, hope, and the unspoken magic of the Christmas season.

Chapter 35: The Snow Globe Mystery

In the heart of the bustling town of Evergreen Falls, the holiday season brought with it an air of enchantment that permeated every corner. Twinkling lights lined the streets, carolers sang joyfully in the square, and snow fell softly from the sky, covering the town in a blanket of white. In the midst of this festive scene stood *Old Holloway's Curiosities*, an antiquated shop that had been part of Evergreen Falls for generations. Inside its dusty windows, treasures from times past glittered in the candlelight, but there was one item in particular that would soon captivate the town—a mysterious snow globe that held the key to an unexpected adventure.

The Discovery of the Snow Globe

Old Holloway's shop had always been a place of wonder, filled with antiques, trinkets, and oddities collected from around the world. But on a chilly December morning, a new item appeared in the window, drawing the attention of every passerby. It was a snow globe, unlike any other. Encased in its glass dome was a perfect replica of Evergreen Falls, complete with the town square, the grand Christmas tree, and even tiny, lifelike figures of townsfolk going about their holiday activities.

Inside the snow globe, snowflakes swirled gently, sparkling like tiny stars in the light. Yet, what truly set this snow globe apart was the peculiar sense of magic that seemed to emanate from it, a sensation that made everyone who gazed upon it feel a strange mixture of awe and curiosity.

"That's a new one, isn't it?" remarked Clara, the shopkeeper's assistant, as she stepped inside the shop that morning. Mr. Holloway, the shop's owner, was arranging a stack of old books on a nearby shelf.

"Indeed," he replied, his eyes twinkling with a hint of mystery. "It arrived yesterday in a shipment from an estate sale, though I don't recall ordering it."

Clara moved closer to examine the snow globe, entranced by the tiny scene within. As she did, she noticed something odd. "Mr. Holloway, look at this," she said, pointing to the base of the globe. There, etched into the brass stand, was an inscription that read: *"Wishes come true, but be careful what you wish for."*

The Snow Globe's Strange Effects

Curious, Clara reached out and gently picked up the snow globe. The moment she held it in her hands, a wave of warmth washed over her, and the snow inside the globe began to swirl faster, almost as if responding to her touch.

"I wish it would stop snowing for a while," she murmured, half-joking, as she gazed into the miniature scene. Evergreen Falls had been blanketed in snow for weeks, and a break from the cold would be a welcome relief.

To her astonishment, the snow within the globe ceased its swirling and settled to the bottom. At the exact same moment, the snow falling outside the shop window stopped abruptly, leaving the town eerily still.

Mr. Holloway, who had been watching from behind the counter, raised an eyebrow. "Interesting," he said slowly. "It seems this snow globe is no ordinary trinket."

Clara felt a shiver run down her spine. Could it be that the snow globe had somehow granted her wish? She set it back on the counter, eyeing it warily. "It must be a coincidence," she muttered, though a part of her wasn't so sure.

A Growing Mystery

Word of the strange snow globe spread quickly through Evergreen Falls. People came to Old Holloway's to see it for themselves, drawn by tales of its supposed magic. Some dismissed the story as nonsense, but others were captivated by the possibility that the globe held a real, mysterious power.

The townsfolk began to notice peculiar things happening around town. Whenever someone in the shop made an idle wish while gazing into the globe, a curious set of events would follow. When little Tommy, a local boy, wished for his missing cat to return, the very next day, the cat was found sitting on the doorstep, meowing as if it had never been lost. When Mrs. Abbott, the florist, wished for more customers, her shop was suddenly flooded with visitors buying flowers for holiday decorations.

Each time, the snow globe's snowflakes would swirl and then settle, as though acknowledging the wish. Mr. Holloway and Clara kept a close eye on the globe, documenting each occurrence. The townsfolk grew excited, whispering among themselves about the snow globe's magic.

However, with the good came the unforeseen. One evening, a group of children, giddy with the holiday spirit, crowded into the shop. Among them was Peter, known for his mischief. He grinned as he picked up the snow globe and declared loudly, "I wish for the biggest snowstorm this town has ever seen!"

The snow within the globe swirled violently, faster than it ever had before. Mr. Holloway gasped. "Put it down, quickly!" he shouted, but it was too late. The storm inside the globe raged, and as the children backed away, the snowflakes outside began to fall thick and fast, casting a heavy, blinding curtain over the town.

The Consequences of the Wish

The snowstorm descended upon Evergreen Falls, fierce and unyielding. By morning, the town was buried under several feet of snow, trapping residents in their homes and halting all holiday activities. Streets were impassable, and businesses remained closed. It was as if the entire town had been frozen in place.

In the days that followed, Mr. Holloway and Clara grew increasingly concerned. "The globe is responding to wishes," Clara said, pacing the shop. "But it seems to take them literally, without regard for the consequences."

"We need to reverse this," Mr. Holloway replied gravely, his eyes fixed on the snow globe. "The question is how."

Clara looked at the snow globe, deep in thought. The inscription on the base echoed in her mind: *"Wishes come true, but be careful what you wish for."* She realized that the globe's magic might require a balance—a wish made in selfishness or haste could lead to unforeseen effects.

"Perhaps," she suggested slowly, "we need to make a wish that comes from the heart, something that restores balance and considers the good of everyone."

The Heartfelt Wish

Determined to set things right, Clara took the snow globe in her hands. The snowflakes inside danced chaotically, mirroring the storm outside. Closing her eyes, she focused on the warmth she felt for the town and its people.

"I wish for peace and warmth to return to Evergreen Falls," she whispered, her voice filled with sincerity. "May the snowstorm ease, and may everyone find joy and comfort this Christmas."

The globe glowed softly, and the swirling snowflakes gradually slowed, settling into a gentle, peaceful drift. Outside, the howling wind died down, and the heavy snowfall turned into a light, delicate flurry. The town, which had been plunged into a deep freeze, now glistened under a clear, serene sky.

As Clara opened her eyes, she noticed a soft, golden glow within the globe. The miniature town inside looked more vibrant, the tiny figures seemed to dance in joy, and a warm light emanated from every window. The snow globe had responded, but this time, it felt different. It was as if the globe had accepted the wish not just as a command, but as an act of care.

The Surprise Ending

The townsfolk emerged cautiously from their homes, marveling at the sudden change in weather. As they gathered in the square, Mr. Holloway and Clara stepped out of the shop, the snow globe in Clara's hands.

"What happened?" people asked, their faces filled with curiosity and wonder.

Clara smiled, holding up the globe for all to see. "The snow globe granted our wishes," she explained. "But it taught us that our wishes have power, and with that power comes responsibility. When we wish for something, we must consider its impact on others."

The townsfolk nodded, understanding now that the magic of the snow globe lay not in granting every desire, but in teaching them to wish thoughtfully and with kindness.

Just as Clara finished speaking, the globe glowed once more, catching everyone's attention. Inside, the snowflakes swirled gently, and a new inscription appeared at the base: *The heart that wishes wisely, wishes for all.*

As the glow faded, a final surprise emerged. Inside the globe, where the tiny town had been, now stood a shimmering Christmas tree, its branches adorned with lights and decorations that twinkled like stars. The townsfolk gasped in delight, recognizing the miniature version of their own town square, now radiating warmth and unity.

Clara glanced up at Mr. Holloway, who gave her a knowing smile. "It seems the globe has given us its final gift," he said softly. "A reminder of the power of community, of thinking beyond ourselves."

From that day on, the snow globe remained in Old Holloway's Curiosities, a cherished artifact that reminded the villagers of the holiday's true magic. Whenever someone came into the shop to make a wish, they were encouraged to hold the globe, reflect on their wish, and consider its impact on the world around them.

The story of the snow globe became a legend in Evergreen Falls, passed down through generations. It was said that the globe still held magic, but only for those who wished with a heart full of love and generosity. And so, every Christmas, the town gathered in the square, not to make wishes for themselves, but to wish for joy, peace, and warmth for one another.

In the end, the mystery of the snow globe was not about the granting of wishes, but about discovering the beauty of thoughtful giving and the joy that comes from a heart that wishes for the happiness of all.

Conclusion: *The Christmas Dawn: New Beginnings and Endings*

Chapter 36: Christmas Morning

The night had finally settled into a hush, blanketing the world in a quiet stillness that only Christmas Eve can bring. Outside, a fresh layer of snow sparkled under the moonlight, casting a soft glow over the village of Maplewood. In the Linwood household, nestled near the edge of the town square, every light was turned off except for the twinkling bulbs on the Christmas tree. Stockings were hung by the fireplace, gifts lay neatly wrapped under the tree, and a sense of anticipation filled the air.

As the first light of dawn peeked through the curtains, Christmas morning arrived with all its magic. For a moment, everything seemed frozen in time, as if the world was holding its breath in awe of the day's beauty. It was the kind of morning that carried with it a promise—a promise of joy, warmth, and the reminder of what truly matters.

The First Awakenings

Inside the Linwood house, the quiet was broken by the sound of small feet tiptoeing down the hallway. It was Lily, the youngest of the family, peeking out from her bedroom to see if the magic had happened overnight. The glow of the Christmas tree greeted her, and her eyes widened at the sight of the gifts piled beneath it. She gasped softly, a smile spreading across her face as the excitement bubbled up inside her.

"Mom! Dad! Wake up!" she called, unable to contain herself any longer. "It's Christmas!"

The house stirred to life. Down the hall, her older siblings, Peter and Emma, woke up with sleepy smiles, the promise of the morning urging them out of bed. Mr. and Mrs. Linwood exchanged a glance and a knowing smile, remembering their own childhood Christmas mornings. They quickly threw on their robes and followed the children into the living room, where the magic of Christmas morning awaited.

Lily was already sitting by the tree, her eyes shining as she took in every ornament, every twinkling light, and the gifts that lay scattered in a beautiful array. For a moment, no one moved. They simply stood together, basking in the warm glow and the profound peace that filled the room.

"Look!" Peter whispered, pointing out the window. The family turned to see the snow-covered landscape outside, glistening in the morning light. It was as if the entire world had been freshly painted, a perfect backdrop to the joy that filled their hearts.

Opening Gifts: A Moment of Joy

"Okay, who wants to go first?" Mrs. Linwood asked, settling down on the couch. The children gathered around the tree, their excitement palpable. It was a family tradition to open gifts one at a time, savoring each moment and each other's reactions.

Lily picked up a small package wrapped in silver paper with a blue ribbon. Her name was written on the tag in Peter's handwriting. She carefully untied the ribbon and peeled back the paper to reveal a tiny glass snow globe. Inside was a miniature Christmas tree surrounded by twinkling stars.

"It's beautiful, Peter!" she exclaimed, hugging her brother tightly. "Thank you!"

Peter smiled, watching his sister's delight. "I knew you loved snow globes," he said. "So I wanted you to have one of your own."

As the unwrapping continued, the room filled with laughter, gratitude, and the simple joy of giving. There were knitted scarves, new books, handmade trinkets, and thoughtful surprises. Each gift, no matter how big or small, carried with it the warmth of love and the careful thought that had gone into choosing or making it.

Mr. Linwood handed a gift to his wife, a small package he had kept tucked away at the back of the tree. As she opened it, her eyes widened. Inside was a delicate gold locket, engraved with the initials of each family member. She opened the locket to find a tiny photo of them all together, taken during their summer holiday.

"It's perfect," she whispered, tears welling up in her eyes. "It's a piece of all of us that I can keep close, always."

The children clapped and cheered, happy to see the joy on their mother's face. And in that moment, the Linwoods felt the true essence of Christmas—love, togetherness, and the joy of sharing meaningful moments with those who matter most.

The Forgotten Ornament Shines Again

After the gifts had been opened, Mr. Linwood picked up the tree's most cherished decoration—the *Forgotten Ornament*, which they had rediscovered earlier in the season. He turned it in his hands, admiring the painted scene of the snow-covered village and the shimmering light it captured.

"Let's hang it together," he said, smiling at his family. "This ornament represents the memories we've made and the new ones we're creating. It's our reminder of what Christmas truly means."

With care, they hung the ornament on a branch near the top of the tree, where it caught the light and sparkled brilliantly. It was as if the ornament came to life, reflecting back the warmth and love that filled the room.

They gathered around the tree, hands clasped, taking in the scene before them. It was not the gifts, the decorations, or even the delicious breakfast waiting in the kitchen that made this morning special. It was the sense of unity, the feeling that in this moment, they were part of something greater—a tradition of love, joy, and giving that transcended time.

A Moment of Reflection

As they settled down on the couch with mugs of hot cocoa, Mr. Linwood cleared his throat. "Every Christmas morning, I like to take a moment to reflect," he began, his voice warm and steady. "It's easy to get caught up in the excitement of gifts and festivities, but the real magic of Christmas lies in what we carry in our hearts."

He looked at each of them, his gaze softening. "This season is about more than just a single day of joy. It's about the spirit of giving, the love we share, and the kindness we show not just to each other, but to everyone around us. It's about taking this warmth and spreading it throughout the year."

Emma nodded thoughtfully. "Like how we helped at the food drive last week," she said, remembering the feeling of handing out meals to families in need.

"Exactly," Mrs. Linwood added. "Christmas isn't just a date on the calendar. It's a reminder of the goodness and generosity that we can practice every day."

Lily, cradling her new snow globe, looked up at her parents. "So, Christmas can happen all year if we keep that spirit?" she asked.

Mr. Linwood smiled, pride shining in his eyes. "Yes, sweetheart. Christmas is in every act of kindness, every moment of giving, and every time we open our hearts to others. That's the true magic of the season."

Carrying the Christmas Spirit Forward

The family sat quietly for a moment, each of them reflecting on the words spoken. It was a simple truth, yet so profound. Christmas wasn't just about the presents, the tree, or the feast that awaited them. It was about the love they shared and the warmth they brought into the world, one small act at a time.

Outside, the village of Maplewood was coming to life. In homes all around, families were sharing their own Christmas mornings, unwrapping gifts, laughing, and creating memories that would last a lifetime. But the magic of the morning went beyond these personal moments. It spread through the streets and into the hearts of everyone, reminding them that the spirit of Christmas was something to be carried with them long after the day itself had passed.

An Invitation to the Year Ahead

As the Linwoods finished their cocoa and began preparing for breakfast, they made a promise to each other—a promise to carry the spirit of Christmas with them throughout the year. They vowed to continue acts of kindness, to find joy in simple moments, and to always be there for one another and their community.

The day was just beginning, filled with the promise of more laughter, more joy, and more memories to be made. But they knew that the real magic of Christmas was already with them, wrapped up in the love that filled their home.

And so, as you finish reading this story, the invitation extends to you as well. Let this Christmas morning be more than a fleeting moment of happiness. Let it be the start of a new tradition of love, kindness, and giving. Carry the warmth of this day into the year ahead, spreading the light of Christmas in every season, with every smile, every act of compassion, and every shared moment of joy.

For Christmas is not just a day; it's a state of heart. It's the gift we give ourselves and each other when we choose to see the world with wonder, to cherish the people around us, and to create a tapestry of memories woven with love.

So, take a deep breath, close your eyes for a moment, and let the magic of Christmas morning fill you. Hold onto it, nurture it, and let it guide you through each day of the coming year. This is the true spirit of Christmas—a light that never dims, a joy that never fades, and a love that grows with every passing moment.

Appendices

Appendix A: Recipes & Crafts Index

This appendix compiles all the recipes and crafts mentioned throughout the book, providing a convenient guide to help you bring the festive spirit of Christmas into your home. From heartwarming recipes to imaginative crafts, each entry here includes a brief description and the chapter in which it appears, allowing you to easily locate the full instructions. This index aims to inspire you to try new holiday activities, create lasting memories, and share the joy of the season with family and friends.

1. Recipes Index

The holiday season is synonymous with delicious treats and warm meals that bring people together. Below is a detailed list of the recipes featured in this book, each accompanied by a short description and where to find it:

Chapter 11: Grandma's Secret Recipe

1. **Mulled Wine**

   A classic spiced wine simmered with cloves, cinnamon, and orange slices, perfect for cozying up on a cold winter's night. This recipe includes tips for creating both alcoholic and non-alcoholic versions to suit all tastes.

2. **Holiday Spice Cookies**

   These cookies are made with a blend of cinnamon, nutmeg, and cloves, topped with a light glaze. Ideal for sharing, they capture the essence of the season in every bite.

3. **Gingerbread Loaf**

   A moist, spicy loaf rich with molasses and ginger. This recipe comes with suggestions for serving, including pairing it with cream cheese frosting or simply enjoying it with a warm cup of tea.

4. **Homemade Eggnog**

A creamy, traditional Christmas drink made with eggs, milk, sugar, and a hint of nutmeg. Includes instructions for both classic and alcohol-free versions.

Chapter 13: Feasts of Yore

1. **Roasted Chestnuts**

Learn the art of roasting chestnuts over an open fire, with tips on selecting the best chestnuts and achieving the perfect texture and flavor.

2. **Victorian Mince Pies**

A twist on a traditional English Christmas dessert, these mince pies feature a spiced fruit filling encased in buttery pastry. This recipe includes instructions for making your own mincemeat filling.

3. **Yule Log Cake (Bûche de Noël)**

A festive chocolate sponge cake rolled with a rich, creamy filling and decorated to resemble a Yule log. Step-by-step instructions include tips for the perfect roll and decorating ideas to make it look like a woodland masterpiece.

4. **Traditional Wassail**

A spiced cider drink steeped in centuries-old tradition. This recipe walks you through creating a warm, fragrant drink to share during caroling or gatherings, complete with serving suggestions.

Chapter 14: Candied Delights

1. **Peppermint Bark**
A layered candy treat featuring dark chocolate, white chocolate, and crushed peppermint. This simple, no-bake recipe is perfect for gifting and adds a refreshing twist to the season's sweet offerings.

2. **Homemade Caramel Apples**
Crisp apples coated in buttery caramel, with options for toppings such as crushed nuts, sprinkles, or a drizzle of chocolate. This recipe provides tips for achieving a smooth caramel coating.

3. **Candied Orange Peels**
Zesty, sweet orange peels candied to perfection. This recipe guides you through the process of making this classic holiday treat, along with suggestions for using them as garnish or adding to baked goods.

Chapter 15: The Mistletoe Kitchen

1. **Mistletoe Punch**
A refreshing holiday punch made with cranberry juice, sparkling water, and fresh mint. Perfect for serving at Christmas parties or cozy family gatherings.

2. **Love-Spiced Hot Chocolate**
A rich hot chocolate infused with a blend of spices believed to bring warmth and love. This recipe offers variations, including dairy-free and vegan options.

2. Crafts Index

Crafting during the Christmas season adds a personal touch to holiday decorations and gifts. This list provides an overview of the crafts detailed in the book, along with brief descriptions and chapter references for easy access.

Chapter 2: The Wishing Tree

1. **Wishing Tree Ornaments**

   Create unique ornaments that double as wish holders for the New Year. This craft includes step-by-step instructions for making paper stars, writing wishes inside them, and hanging them on your Christmas tree.

Chapter 8: St. Nicholas' Day

1. **St. Nicholas Goodie Bags**

   Small, handcrafted bags filled with treats to celebrate St. Nicholas' Day. This craft includes a simple sewing pattern for making the bags and ideas for filling them with traditional candies, nuts, and small toys.

Chapter 9: The Evergreen's Tale

1. **DIY Wreaths and Garlands**

   Instructions for creating natural wreaths and garlands using pinecones, evergreen branches, berries, and ribbons. Includes tips on weaving in twinkling lights and other decorative elements.

Chapter 12: The Gingerbread Chronicles

1. Gingerbread Houses

A guide to baking and assembling your own gingerbread house, with tips for designing, decorating, and making royal icing to hold everything together. This chapter also includes ideas for creating an entire gingerbread village.

Chapter 14: Candied Delights

1. Candy Cane Place Card Holders

Craft instructions for making festive place card holders using candy canes and ribbon. These simple yet elegant holders add a personal touch to your holiday table setting.

Chapter 16: The Enchanted Forest

1. Pinecone Elves and Fairies

Instructions for crafting adorable pinecone elves and fairies using natural materials like acorns, pinecones, felt, and twine. This project is perfect for families and adds a whimsical touch to your Christmas decor.

Chapter 18: The Secret of Snowflakes

1. Paper Snowflakes

Detailed instructions for creating intricate paper snowflakes, including advanced techniques for adding a three-dimensional effect. This craft is suitable for all ages and can be used to decorate windows, walls, or the Christmas tree.

Chapter 24: The Sleeping Snowman

1. **DIY Snow Globes**
   Learn how to create your own snow globes using mason jars, figurines, and glitter. This craft includes tips for choosing the best
   materials, sealing the jars, and adding personal touches.

Chapter 28: Winter Wonderland Crafts

1. **Cinnamon Stick Candle Holders**
   A simple yet fragrant craft involving cinnamon sticks, small pillar
   candles, and ribbon. This guide provides step-by-step instructions for creating a cozy, rustic centerpiece for your holiday table.
2. **Crystal Snowflake Ornaments**
   Instructions for making sparkling snowflake ornaments using
   pipe cleaners and borax crystals. This craft involves an overnight
   process that results in beautiful, crystalline decorations for your
   tree.
3. **Woodland Creature Ornaments**
   Felt ornaments shaped like woodland creatures such as foxes,
   owls, and deer. This craft includes patterns and sewing tips to create charming, nature-inspired decorations.

Chapter 33: The Book of Wishes

1. **Creating Your Book of Wishes**
   A guide to making a personalized Book of Wishes using a journal
   or handmade booklet. Includes tips for decorating the cover, organizing sections for different types of wishes, and incorporating
   reflective rituals.

Tips for Successful Holiday Crafting and Baking

- **Plan Ahead:** Many holiday crafts and recipes require time and patience. Make a list of the materials and ingredients you'll need beforehand to avoid last-minute stress.

- **Get the Whole Family Involved:** Crafting and baking can be enjoyable activities for all ages. Assign roles to family members, whether it's measuring ingredients, cutting paper, or decorating cookies.

- **Experiment with Personal Touches:** While the provided instructions serve as a guide, feel free to add your unique spin to each recipe and craft. Incorporate family traditions or favorite ingredients to make each creation truly special.

- **Share the Joy:** Use these crafts and recipes to create gifts for friends, neighbors, or those in need. A handmade ornament or a tin of holiday cookies can brighten someone's day and spread the spirit of Christmas.

This index is meant to inspire and guide you in your holiday preparations, allowing you to make the most of the season's magic. Whether you're whipping up a batch of gingerbread cookies or crafting a pinecone elf with your children, remember that the true essence of Christmas lies not in perfection, but in the joy of creating and sharing with others. Happy crafting and baking!

Appendix B: Traditions Around the World

Christmas is celebrated around the world in diverse and colorful ways, each culture bringing its own unique customs and traditions to the holiday season. From vibrant parades to quiet, candlelit services, these traditions capture the spirit of Christmas in all its warmth, joy, and wonder. This appendix explores some of the most enchanting and distinctive Christmas customs from different cultures, offering a glimpse into the many ways people celebrate this special time of year.

1. Germany: Weihnachtsmarkt and Advent

Germany is known for its enchanting *Weihnachtsmarkt* (Christmas markets) that pop up in towns and cities throughout December. These markets are filled with wooden stalls selling handcrafted ornaments, candles, and other holiday trinkets. The air is fragrant with the scent of roasted chestnuts, mulled wine (Glühwein), and spiced gingerbread (Lebkuchen). Visitors often stroll through the market with a warm cup of Glühwein, soaking in the festive atmosphere.

Another key tradition in Germany is the *Advent season*. Many families use Advent calendars filled with small gifts or chocolates to count down the days until Christmas. A popular custom is the *Advent wreath* (Adventskranz), a circular wreath with four candles. Each Sunday in Advent, a candle is lit, symbolizing the light and joy that Christmas brings.

How to Incorporate This Tradition: Create your own Advent calendar or wreath to count down to Christmas. Fill the calendar with small treats, inspirational quotes, or simple activities to do each day.

2. Sweden: St. Lucia's Day (Luciadagen)

In Sweden, the Christmas season begins on December 13th with *St. Lucia's Day*, a festival of light in the middle of the dark Scandinavian winter. St. Lucia was a Christian martyr, and her feast day is celebrated with processions led by a girl chosen to represent St. Lucia. She wears a white robe and a crown of candles, symbolizing light and hope.

During the procession, children dress in white robes, carrying candles and singing traditional songs. The procession moves through schools, churches, and even homes, bringing warmth and light to the community. Families often celebrate by baking saffron buns called *Lussekatter* and serving them with coffee or mulled wine.

How to Incorporate This Tradition: Light candles on December 13th and enjoy a warm treat like saffron buns or gingerbread cookies with your family. Take a moment to appreciate the light in the midst of winter's darkness.

3. Mexico: Las Posadas

In Mexico, Christmas celebrations begin on December 16th with *Las Posadas*, a nine-day event that reenacts Mary and Joseph's search for shelter in Bethlehem. Each night, families and friends form a procession, carrying candles and singing carols as they move from house to house. At each stop, they reenact the scene of Mary and Joseph asking for a place to stay. The hosts deny them entry until the final house, where they are welcomed in for a festive celebration.

The evening ends with a party, featuring music, dancing, and traditional foods such as tamales and *atole* (a warm, sweet drink made from corn). A piñata, often shaped like a star, is hung up for children to break open, showering them with candy and small toys.

How to Incorporate This Tradition: Host a small gathering where family and friends reenact a procession, singing carols and lighting candles. End with a cozy dinner of traditional Mexican dishes or break open a piñata filled with treats for the children.

4. Italy: La Befana and the Feast of the Seven Fishes

In Italy, Christmas celebrations extend into January with the arrival of *La Befana*, a kindly old witch who delivers gifts to children on Epiphany Eve (January 5th). According to legend, La Befana was invited by the Wise Men to visit the baby Jesus, but she declined, saying she was too busy. Later, realizing her mistake, she set out to find the Christ child, bringing gifts for all the children she encountered. Today, Italian children hang stockings in hopes of receiving sweets from La Befana, while naughty children may find lumps of coal.

Another cherished Italian Christmas tradition is the *Feast of the Seven Fishes* (La Vigilia), celebrated on Christmas Eve. Families prepare a meal featuring a variety of seafood dishes, often including eel, clams, shrimp, and baccalà (salted cod). This feast is a symbolic fast from meat in anticipation of the birth of Christ.

How to Incorporate This Tradition: Create your own version of a seafood feast on Christmas Eve, or prepare a simpler Italian meal using family-favorite recipes. Share the story of La Befana with children and invite them to hang stockings on Epiphany Eve.

5. Philippines: Simbang Gabi and the Giant Lantern Festival

In the Philippines, Christmas is celebrated with *Simbang Gabi*, a series of nine dawn masses held from December 16th to December 24th. The masses are a way for Filipinos to express their devotion and prepare spiritually for Christmas. Churches are adorned with colorful lanterns, and families gather afterward to share traditional Filipino treats such as *puto bumbong* (purple rice cakes) and *bibingka* (rice cakes with coconut).

One of the most spectacular events in the Philippines is the *Giant Lantern Festival* (Ligligan Parul) held in the city of San Fernando. Enormous, intricately designed lanterns light up the night, symbolizing the star of Bethlehem and the spirit of hope and joy.

How to Incorporate This Tradition: Attend an early morning or evening mass during the Christmas season, or simply light candles at home to create a sense of peace and reflection. Try making or purchasing traditional Filipino Christmas treats to enjoy with family.

6. Iceland: The Yule Lads and the Christmas Book Flood

In Iceland, Christmas is marked by the visit of the *Yule Lads*, thirteen mischievous but good-hearted trolls who come down from the mountains in the thirteen days leading up to Christmas. Each night, children place a shoe on their windowsill, and the Yule Lads leave small gifts or candy for those who have been good, or a potato for those who have not.

Another beloved tradition in Iceland is the *Christmas Book Flood* (Jólabókaflóð). Icelanders exchange books as gifts on Christmas Eve and then spend the night reading them, often while enjoying hot cocoa. This tradition reflects Iceland's strong literary culture and the joy of sharing stories.

How to Incorporate This Tradition: Introduce a family book exchange on Christmas Eve. Select books thoughtfully for each family member, then spend the evening reading together with mugs of hot cocoa.

7. Japan: Christmas Eve and KFC Feast

In Japan, Christmas is celebrated as a secular holiday that focuses on spreading happiness and love. One unique tradition is the *Christmas Eve KFC Feast*. In the 1970s, a successful marketing campaign by KFC branded fried chicken as a Christmas meal, and it quickly became a popular tradition. Today, families and couples often enjoy a KFC meal on Christmas Eve, along with a Christmas cake, usually a sponge cake with strawberries and whipped cream.

Christmas in Japan is also a romantic holiday. Couples exchange gifts and spend time together, often viewing Christmas lights and enjoying special dinners.

How to Incorporate This Tradition: Host a fun and lighthearted Christmas Eve dinner with takeout fried chicken or a homemade version. Follow it up with a dessert of strawberry shortcake or another sweet treat.

8. Australia: Christmas Barbecue and Carols by Candlelight

In Australia, Christmas falls in the middle of summer, so the holiday is celebrated outdoors with beach trips, barbecues, and picnics. Families gather for a festive barbecue featuring grilled meats, seafood, and summer salads. The warm weather allows for activities such as swimming, cricket, and backyard games.

A cherished tradition is *Carols by Candlelight*, where communities gather in parks and public spaces to sing Christmas carols by candlelight. This event often takes place on Christmas Eve and includes concerts, performances, and the magic of thousands of candles illuminating the night.

How to Incorporate This Tradition: If you live in a warmer climate, consider hosting a Christmas barbecue with family and friends. Organize a small carol-singing event in your backyard or join a community carol service, lighting candles to create a festive, warm atmosphere.

9. Norway: Julenissen and the Yule Goat

In Norway, the Christmas season is filled with folklore and ancient traditions. One of the most well-known figures is *Julenissen*, a gnome-like creature who brings gifts to children. Julenissen is often depicted with a red cap and a long beard, similar to Santa Claus, but rooted in Norse mythology. Children leave out porridge for Julenissen to keep him happy and ensure they receive gifts.

Another traditional symbol in Norway is the *Yule Goat* (Julebukk). Made of straw and adorned with red ribbons, the Yule Goat is a festive decoration that hearkens back to pagan times. It is sometimes brought to homes by costumed "goat riders" who sing carols and receive treats in return.

How to Incorporate This Tradition: Craft your own Yule Goat using straw or craft materials and place it as a centerpiece in your home. Share the story of Julenissen with children and encourage them to leave out a small bowl of porridge as part of their Christmas Eve preparations.

10. Ukraine: Christmas Eve and the Feast of Sviat Vechir

In Ukraine, Christmas Eve, known as *Sviat Vechir* (Holy Evening), is a time of deep religious significance and family gathering. The centerpiece of the celebration is a twelve-course meal, each dish representing one of Christ's apostles. Traditional foods include *kutia* (a sweet grain pudding), borscht, and varenyky (dumplings). Before the meal, a special prayer is said, and an extra place is often set at the table for the spirits of deceased family members.

A unique aspect of Ukrainian Christmas is the use of spider web ornaments in the Christmas tree. According to folklore, a poor widow could not afford to decorate her tree, but on Christmas morning, it was found covered in webs spun by spiders. The webs turned to silver and gold, bringing prosperity to her family. Today, it is considered good luck to find a spider or spider web on the Christmas tree.

How to Incorporate This Tradition: Prepare a simple but meaningful Christmas Eve meal with dishes that have significance to your family. Craft spider web ornaments from string or yarn to hang on your tree, embracing the idea of unexpected blessings and good fortune.

In Conclusion

This diverse array of Christmas customs highlights the universal themes of love, joy, hope, and community that are celebrated across cultures. Each tradition, whether ancient or modern, speaks to the heart of the season—the spirit of giving, togetherness, and reflection.

As you explore these traditions, consider incorporating one or two into your holiday celebrations. Embracing the customs of different cultures not only enriches your own experience of Christmas but also fosters a sense of global unity and appreciation for the many ways we express the magic of the season. May these traditions inspire you to celebrate the holidays with warmth, joy, and an open heart.

Appendix C: Acknowledgments

Creating this book has been a journey through the magical world of Christmas, filled with heartwarming stories, cherished traditions, and delightful recipes that celebrate the true essence of the holiday season. This appendix is dedicated to acknowledging the sources of inspiration, the contributors, and the timeless customs that have enriched these pages. Without the collective wisdom and creativity of storytellers, bakers, historians, family traditions, and cultural practices, this book would not have been possible.

1. Inspirations for Stories and Themes

The stories woven into this book have been inspired by various cultural legends, folktales, and childhood memories. The rich tapestry of Christmas lore around the world has provided a wealth of inspiration, and I am deeply grateful to the following:

- **Traditional Christmas Tales:** The heartwarming themes and motifs of classic Christmas stories such as *A Christmas Carol* by Charles Dickens, *The Nutcracker* by E.T.A. Hoffmann, and *The Night Before Christmas* by Clement Clarke Moore have greatly influenced the narrative elements in chapters like "The Silent Night," "Yuletide Spirits," and "The Wishing Tree." These timeless works have helped shape the way we view Christmas as a season of wonder, reflection, and joy.

- **Folklore and Cultural Legends:** The magical characters featured in chapters like "The Yule Lads" and "La Befana" were inspired by Icelandic and Italian folklore, respectively. I express deep gratitude to the diverse cultures around the world whose traditions and stories have been preserved through generations, offering a rich source of inspiration for "St. Lucia's Day," "Las Posadas," "The Yule Goat," and more. The variety and depth of global Christmas lore have made it possible to explore the holiday season in such a multifaceted way.

- **Personal Family Traditions:** Many of the stories and activities in this book were inspired by the traditions of my own family. From the joy of baking cookies to the excitement of opening gifts on Christmas morning, these personal experiences have added an authentic and heartfelt touch to the chapters. I would like to thank my family for their love, encouragement, and the memories we have created together over the years. Your warmth and spirit have been the foundation of this book.

- **The Imaginations of Children:** The whimsical and magical elements of Christmas captured in chapters like "The Sleeping Snowman," "The Gingerbread Chronicles," and "The Great Snowball Fight" owe their existence to the boundless imagination of children. I am thankful to the countless children who continue to dream, believe, and bring a sense of wonder to the holiday season. Your joy and curiosity are what keep the magic of Christmas alive.

2. Acknowledgment of Cultural and Historical Resources

This book explores the traditions and practices of Christmas celebrations from various cultures, and I am indebted to the authors, researchers, and historians who have documented these customs. The following resources were instrumental in providing a deeper understanding of global Christmas traditions:

- **Cultural Christmas Studies:** Works such as *The Oxford Companion to Christmas* and *Christmas Around the World* offered invaluable insights into the diverse ways Christmas is celebrated globally. These books provided a solid foundation for chapters like "Christmas Markets," "St. Nicholas' Day," and "Traditions Around the World."

- **Ethnographic Research:** Various ethnographic writings on Christmas traditions in Scandinavia, Latin America, Eastern Europe, and other regions provided detailed descriptions of customs like Sweden's *Sankta Lucia* and Mexico's *Las Posadas*. The stories in this book were greatly enriched by these detailed cultural insights, which helped capture the essence of each tradition.

- **Holiday Crafting and Decorating Guides:** The craft instructions throughout this book, especially in chapters like "Winter Wonderland Crafts," "The Secret of Snowflakes," and "The Enchanted Forest," were influenced by numerous crafting books and online resources dedicated to holiday decor. I extend thanks to crafting communities and authors who have shared their ideas, techniques, and passion for handmade holiday decorations.

3. Recipe Inspirations and Contributions

Food is a central part of Christmas celebrations, and the recipes featured in this book have been inspired by a variety of sources, including family recipes, traditional holiday fare, and the culinary traditions of different cultures. I wish to express my gratitude to the following:

- **Family and Friends:** Many of the recipes in this book, such as "Grandma's Mulled Wine" and "Holiday Spice Cookies," come from family kitchens where holiday gatherings were filled with the aroma of freshly baked goods and warm beverages. I thank my family and friends who have generously shared their recipes, tips, and cooking secrets. Your love of food and hospitality has brought warmth to these pages.
- **Traditional Christmas Cookbooks:** The recipes for "Yule Log Cake," "Victorian Mince Pies," and "Traditional Wassail" were inspired by historical cookbooks and guides that delve into the culinary heritage of Christmas. Books like *Mrs. Beeton's Christmas Recipes* and *Traditional Christmas Cooking* provided the foundation for adapting classic dishes to fit modern kitchens.
- **International Cuisine Sources:** I extend my gratitude to the authors of various international cookbooks and food blogs who have documented the holiday foods of their cultures. Recipes

such as "Saffron Buns" for St. Lucia's Day, "Feast of the Seven Fishes," and Filipino *puto bumbong* owe their authenticity to the careful research and passion for culinary tradition shared by these authors. Your work has helped celebrate the global diversity of Christmas feasts.

4. Artistic and Crafting Influences

The crafting instructions and creative projects featured in this book have been shaped by countless artisans, crafters, and DIY enthusiasts who have shared their talents with the world. I would like to acknowledge:

- **Crafting Communities:** Online communities, such as Pinterest boards, crafting blogs, and DIY websites, have been a wellspring of inspiration for projects like "Paper Snowflakes," "DIY Snow Globes," and "Crystal Snowflake Ornaments." I am grateful to the crafters who share their tutorials, ideas, and enthusiasm for making Christmas a season of creativity.
- **Seasonal Decor Shops:** Visits to local holiday markets and decor shops sparked many of the craft ideas presented in this book. From wreath-making to creating personalized ornaments, the artisans who showcase their work each year inspire countless individuals to bring the magic of the season into their homes.

5. Special Thanks to the Readers

This book would not exist without the spirit and enthusiasm of readers who continue to seek the magic, warmth, and joy of Christmas in its many forms. Your love of stories, traditions, and the holiday season itself is what makes Christmas such a special time of year. I thank you for embarking on this journey with me, for keeping the magic alive, and for your desire to make each Christmas a season of love, generosity, and reflection.

6. Dedication to the Spirit of Christmas

Lastly, this book is dedicated to the *spirit of Christmas* itself—the spirit that lives in the quiet moments of giving, in the laughter shared over a warm meal, in the sparkle of lights on a tree, and in the joy of creating memories with loved ones. This spirit transcends cultures, languages, and traditions, binding us together in a shared celebration of love, hope, and togetherness. May this book serve as a humble tribute to the magic of the season and inspire you to carry its light with you throughout the year.

In crafting this book, I have endeavored to honor the diverse traditions, stories, and joys of Christmas. While not exhaustive, this acknowledgment aims to credit the multitude of sources that have contributed to its creation. It is my hope that you, dear reader, find as much warmth, joy, and inspiration within these pages as I did in bringing them to life.

With heartfelt gratitude,
Matthew Petchinsky

<u>Message from the Author:</u>

I hope you enjoyed this book, I love astrology and knew there was not a book such as this out on the shelf. I love metaphysical items as well. Please check out my other books:

-Life of Government Benefits

-My life of Hell

-My life with Hydrocephalus

-Red Sky

-World Domination:Woman's rule

-World Domination:Woman's Rule 2: The War

-Life and Banishment of Apophis: book 1

-The Kidney Friendly Diet

-The Ultimate Hemp Cookbook

-Creating a Dispensary(legally)

-Cleanliness throughout life: the importance of showering from childhood to adulthood.

-Strong Roots: The Risks of Overcoddling children

-Hemp Horoscopes: Cosmic Insights and Earthly Healing

- Celestial Hemp Navigating the Zodiac: Through the Green Cosmos

-Astrological Hemp: Aligning The Stars with Earth's Ancient Herb

-The Astrological Guide to Hemp: Stars, Signs, and Sacred Leaves

-Green Growth: Innovative Marketing Strategies for your Hemp Products and Dispensary

-Cosmic Cannabis

-Astrological Munchies

-Henry The Hemp

-Zodiacal Roots: The Astrological Soul Of Hemp

- **Green Constellations: Intersection of Hemp and Zodiac**

-Hemp in The Houses: An astrological Adventure Through The Cannabis Galaxy

-Galactic Ganja Guide

Heavenly Hemp

Zodiac Leaves

Doctor Who Astrology

Cannastrology

Stellar Satvias and Cosmic Indicas

<u>Celestial Cannabis: A Zodiac Journey</u>

AstroHerbology: The Sky and The Soil: Volume 1

AstroHerbology:Celestial Cannabis:Volume 2

Cosmic Cannabis Cultivation

The Starry Guide to Herbal Harmony: Volume 1

The Starry Guide to Herbal Harmony: Cannabis Universe: Volume 2

Yugioh Astrology: Astrological Guide to Deck, Duels and more

Nightmare Mansion: Echoes of The Abyss

Nightmare Mansion 2: Legacy of Shadows

Nightmare Mansion 3: Shadows of the Forgotten

Nightmare Mansion 4: Echoes of the Damned

The Life and Banishment of Apophis: Book 2

Nightmare Mansion: Halls of Despair

<u>Healing with Herb: Cannabis and Hydrocephalus</u>

<u>Planetary Pot: Aligning with Astrological Herbs: Volume 1</u>

Fast Track to Freedom: 30 Days to Financial Independence Using AI, Assets, and Agile Hustles

<u>Cosmic Hemp Pathways</u>

How to Become Financially Free in 30 Days: 10,000 Paths to Prosperity

Zodiacal Herbage: Astrological Insights: Volume 1

Nightmare Mansion: Whispers in the Walls

The Daleks Invade Atlantis

Henry the hemp and Hydrocephalus

10X The Kidney Friendly Diet
Cannabis Universe: Adult coloring book
Hemp Astrology: The Healing Power of the Stars
Zodiacal Herbage: Astrological Insights: Cannabis Universe: Volume 2
<u>Planetary Pot: Aligning with Astrological Herbs: Cannabis Universes: Volume 2</u>
Doctor Who Meets the Replicators and SG-1: The Ultimate Battle for Survival
Nightmare Mansion: Curse of the Blood Moon
<u>The Celestial Stoner: A Guide to the Zodiac</u>
Cosmic Pleasures: Sex Toy Astrology for Every Sign
Hydrocephalus Astrology: Navigating the Stars and Healing Waters
Lapis and the Mischievous Chocolate Bar

Celestial Positions: Sexual Astrology for Every Sign
Apophis's Shadow Work Journal: : A Journey of Self-Discovery and Healing
Kinky Cosmos: Sexual Kink Astrology for Every Sign
Digital Cosmos: The Astrological Digimon Compendium
Stellar Seeds: The Cosmic Guide to Growing with Astrology
Apophis's Daily Gratitude Journal

Cat Astrology: Feline Mysteries of the Cosmos
The Cosmic Kama Sutra: An Astrological Guide to Sexual Positions
Unleash Your Potential: A Guided Journal Powered by AI Insights
Whispers of the Enchanted Grove

Cosmic Pleasures: An Astrological Guide to Sexual Kinks
369, 12 Manifestation Journal

Whisper of the nocturne journal(blank journal for writing or drawing)

The Boogey Book

Locked In Reflection: A Chastity Journey Through Locktober

Generating Wealth Quickly:

How to Generate $100,000 in 24 Hours

Star Magic: Harness the Power of the Universe

The Flatulence Chronicles: A Fart Journal for Self-Discovery

The Doctor and The Death Moth

Seize the Day: A Personal Seizure Tracking Journal

The Ultimate Boogeyman Safari: A Journey into the Boogie World and Beyond

Whispers of Samhain: 1,000 Spells of Love, Luck, and Lunar Magic: Samhain Spell Book

Apophis's guides:

Witch's Spellbook Crafting Guide for Halloween

<u>Frost & Flame: The Enchanted Yule Grimoire of 1000 Winter Spells</u>

<u>The Ultimate Boogey Goo Guide & Spooky Activities for Halloween Fun</u>

Harmony of the Scales: A Libra's Spellcraft for Balance and Beauty

If you want solar for your home go here: https://www.harborsolar.live/apophisenterprises/

Get Some Tarot cards: https://www.makeplayingcards.com/sell/apophis-occult-shop

Get some shirts: https://www.bonfire.com/store/apophis-shirt-emporium/

<u>**Instagrams:**</u>
@apophis_enterprises,
@apophisbookemporium,
@apophisscardshop
Twitter: @apophisenterpr1
 Tiktok:@apophisenterprise
Youtube: @sg1fan23477, @FiresideRetreatKingdom

Podcast: Apophis Chat Zone: https://open.spotify.com/show/ 5zXbrCLEV2xzCp8ybrfHsk?si=fb4d4fdbdce44dec

Newsletter: https://apophiss-newsletter-27c897.beehiiv.com/